Cover Letters

3 Manuscripts in 1 Book, Including: How to Write a Cover Letter, How to Write a Resume and How to Develop Your Career

Theodore Kingsley

D1524992

More by Theodore Kingsley

Discover all books from the Career Development Series by
Theodore Kingsley at:

bit.ly/theodore-kingsley

Book 1: How to Write a Resume

Book 2: How to Write a Cover Letter

Book 3: How to Find a Job

Book 4: How to Prepare for Job Interviews

Book 5: How to Brand Yourself

Book 6: How to Network

Book 7: How to Develop Your Career

Book 8: How to Change Careers

Themed book bundles available at discounted prices:

bit.ly/theodore-kingsley

Copyright

Table of Contents

Book 1: How to Write a Cover Letter

7 Easy Steps to Master Cover Letters, Motivation Letter Examples & Writing Job Applications

Theodore Kingsley

Introduction

Welcome to How to Write a Cover Letter. So the time has come to make a cover letter. Maybe you always like putting your best foot forward, or perhaps the job in question is your dream, and you're polishing your presentation like never before. Whatever your motivation, the time has come to craft, hone and revise and otherwise perfect the first thing an interviewer will likely read. With the economies often as turbulent as white-water rapids and businesses as unreliable as the classic rope bridge over those churning waters, it can pay big to master the humble cover letter.

When prospective hires are equal, your resume is weak, or your background is not reflective of your desired future, learning how to create a compelling page of your personal mission and how it intersects with the company is crucial to gaining a foothold.

As you go through the chapters, keep a sample cover letter handy and update it as we go. The key to *any* excellent creative project is revision and revising. While you want to customize your cover letters to the posted job specifically, much of the content is formulaic and can be used almost universally. Do not worry; we will examine the various themes, pitches, and formats you can use to make your case, breaking down concepts and ideas so you have a complete toolbox.

When your dream job is the possible prize, no effort is wasted. So get a blank document open and consider where you want to be in five years.

Let's get started!

Chapter 1: Step 1 - Learn Cover Letter Basics

The cover letter is either ignored entirely or becomes as important as the resume, curriculum vitae, or other personnel content it fronts. While a lot can hinge on the cover letter, the format is relatively unchanging so that you can perfect its layout and content; we know what the reader expects to see, and you can find out what they want to see. With just a little bit of fine-tuning, yours can be a standout.

At first blush, the cover letter is simple. It's brief, only one page, and contains your mission statement and some professional highlights or unique skill sets. Like anything small but significant, its simplicity creates complexity when we have such a limited space to convey so much. The cover letter is where you sell yourself, target the specific job and position, then make any necessary personal appeals (hint: playing on emotions is never recommended). Ultimately, the cover letter should trigger positive feedback in the reader, even if auto sorted beforehand.

Universal Letter Format

The cover letter follows the outline of handwritten letters from the days of yore, with a few distinct differences. Format the page to standard printer paper, 8.5 x 11, on a white background with a black, easy-to-read font. As a glance, the contact info is separate from the main body; the main body has three distinct parts, with the greeting and signature lines bracketing the primary content on the top and bottom.

While occasionally an office might ask you to print a hard copy, for the most part, modern office environments are going 100% digital, or at least as much as possible.

Any divination from the norm must serve the objective: a cover letter is not the place to express yourself, at least not beyond the narrow scope of a quick correspondence. Colors, rich text, and graphics are too much; save those embellishments for the resume or whatever content the cover letter is fronting.

Fun with Fonts

As much as we all love to play around with fonts, functionality wins out over personal expression every time in a professional setting. San serif fonts can be hard to read over long periods, but a cover letter's single page makes the modern fonts okay. Times New Roman is still a classic, though Veranda and Arial are fine choices, too. Suppose you are going for a design or creative job or just really want to focus on the details. In that case, you may wish to fill blocks of text with Lorem Script (free, online Lorem generators give you endless random gibberish words to fill sample text blocks) to see how different fonts look at a glance. Agonizing over font is as natural as a bridezilla and her wedding dress to folks who love typography. Still, the cover letter is at least practical- Focus on professionalism and readability.

Contact Details

List your contact details first, *including the hiring manager, HR, or hiring department's address.* Including the recipient makes sure your content makes it to the right place and you to them in the mind of the screener. Right indent this section or otherwise set it apart from the main body of content. Some designer formats go so far as to place their info in a color box or bar, but that might be *over-design* in most bossiness settings.

Name, phone number, address without house numbers, email, and any relevant websites. Use your full name, no nicknames or informal abbreviations. Only include a business line if they are both labeled, and the business line is exclusive to you. The address should be scrubbed of house numbers and capable of receiving mail addressed to you. Make sure your email address is professional and, again, accessible to you. Websites need to be professional and *directly* related to your fields, like portfolios and academic profiles; even something general like LinkedIn or Indeed should only be included if examples of your professional work are needed.

Salutation

The **salutation** differs by context, but the classic "dear" is standard, even in formal business settings. You may want to alter the next word on a case-by-case basis, as you will occasionally have the opportunity to make things more specific. If you do not know the details of the hiring department, stick with "Dear Hiring Manager" or "Dear [company name] Recruiter." Be as particular as you can, and entering the person's name that you know processes your content is encouraged if you have that information.

Introduction and Self-promotion

The **introduction and self-promotion** should go in the same sentence, first thing. After the salutation, introduce yourself and state why you are the best pick for the job. Note keywords from the job posting and include them, too. There's no way to overstate the importance of the first sentence- feel free to agonize over it the way you might a love letter to your true love, without the romance, using a keyword or two from the job description as you would a lovers name. As much as I don't want to wax poetic in a professional development setting, the initial words are crucial.

If this is a lateral transition, which means you're using the same skill set between your last job and the next, this line should focus on what essential skills or unique abilities you bring to the task. If it's a pivotal change, new skills, or significant tasks not reflected in your job history, this line needs to bait *and* set the hook.

Name who refereed you or gave you a reference. "John Doe indicated I might be a good fit for this position" or similar name drop is encouraged as long as the person vouching for you is themselves a solid individual. I have found myself stuck between wanting a contact in a company and knowing said individual was something of a flake. Sometimes the person we know socially is an altogether different person at work, so always think twice when it comes to claiming a personal reference.

Stating an achievement makes a good impression, along the lines of "at Xyz Corp, I oversaw systems changes that increased efficiency by 15%" sounds like a cold open but works excellent for a cover letter. At best, you want to stick to recorded or officially verified accomplishments, as the hiring person may check while contacting references. If you are prone to understatement, try a few self-aggrandizing lines to limber up, then dial it back to something "merely" grand. If you tend toward the superlative anyway, make sure you are not coming across as smug, arrogant, or condescending.

Be aware of your strengths, don't assume mastery but project confidence and knowledge. Avoid playing on feelings except where they might contribute to your plea- *everyone* will be passionate about the position or company. Any emotional argument should be in the middle or last section of the main body, if at all.

Remember to **use a keyword or two from the job post**: many companies use automated programs to pre-screen applications and

14

cover letters, and SEO (Search engine optimization) techniques work here, too.

Main Body

The **main body** should consist of three paragraphs worth of text, broken up into more but never less: *avoid the dreaded Block Of Text* in all your written communications. The paragraph break is a beautiful way to break up information and give the eyes a break. While you don't have to be quite as precise in that golden first sentence, you should remain concise and passionate while being thorough and professional.

The second paragraph should focus on your intent. Following the introduction, the intent section should flow naturally from the greeting. In the second paragraph, you begin to showcase the professional and relevant traits you bring to the team, ensuring it's related to the target profession.

If you go more than three paragraphs, make them small and stay on target. You need to have room in the cover letter for **a conclusion**, where you restate your highlights and drive home your agenda. The conclusion should be almost as punchy as the first sentence, a dazzling and concise summation of the whole. You are selling yourself, so taking the *Always Be Closing* mentality to the cover letter is OK if you're not obnoxious about it. "I am excited to join the team!" or "I would love the chance to discuss what contributions I can make to the company!" carry a good deal of confidence and assure the reader you are happy to become a part of a whole.

Be sure the last thing they read is a request for a reply back. It doesn't matter if it's to schedule an interview or give their condolences; make sure you request they get in touch with you. While they may not (busy or apathetic), it is often simply a matter of reminding a busy person to click a button.

Signature

Last, the signature follows all. Name, title, and email address are the usual content. While there are ways to insert your actual signature, best practices are used to demand you NOT use your own signature and just insert a generic handwriting-like font. The number of places that allow fraudulently used signatures to seal a deal is dwindling fast, and identity theft remediation gets faster and quicker every year. Still, there's no need to take chances, and there are web services that notarize and vouch for signatures.

While your signed name is essential, the signature line has recently taken up the herald or even postscript role: a short personal statement or final call for action is not uncommon here, even in personal emails.

In your word processing software or email provider, look for a Signature Line as a drop-in, usually under the Insert option. Make sure your email is correct all the information is entered correctly.

Adding a **short statement of some kind** can go below all of that. Still, *you should remain hesitant to do so*: just like postscripts went obsolete because editing in a digital medium makes them unnecessary, any content you might want to stick in the signature block *should* just go in the main body. However, as a matter of personal expression or final word, it might be an area worth populating. If the work environment or application screener is a known entity, throwing a final spin on your cover letter can make it stand out.

The cover letter is your foot in the door, your first impression, and a fast-talking burst of enthusiastic declarations all rolled into one. Use the detailed style guide further on to fine-tune your message. I have used that expression before because, just like a performance sports car, you need a cover letter to win a race, and in the case of a large company experiencing growth, you can have hundreds of competitors.

Chapter 2: Step 2 - Brush Up on Style

Now that you have the content lined up, it's time for the revision pass. An essential step in anything you create that needs to carry weight, any first draft is going to be inferior to what you get after a few versions of editing. Note: you are not starting over at every step; the days of baskets full of paper from unsatisfactory editions are long past. Make the most of the digital medium by keeping multiple cover letter versions available. Looking forward, chapter three goes over what types of cover letters you may need, so think about them in terms of templates and forms you can customize instead of stand-alone missives.

Excitement and Confidence

Make sure your delivery is upbeat and leaves no room for doubt. You don't "think" you would be a perfect match for the job. You "know" you would. State your best, most relevant skills and traits first, make sure every paragraph pops and bounces. A paragraph pops when every word carries essential information and bounces when one section ends on an allusion to the next.

You can get too much energy into a body of text, so break toward professional and polite when in doubt. If looking for stylistic inspiration, think of an inspirational or motivational speaker like Tony Robbins: never dull, but never strays off-topic. Since you can't very well read it to them in a cheerful voice, *use a short, concise sentence structure to make the words read fast.*

In fact, reading a cover letter out loud can help you iron outflow, style, and content. Imagine the hiring personnel in front of you, maybe even pull up the website and pull up the headshot of someone you might talk to or even just their building or logo to inspire you. Hearing the words aloud forces you to appraise them differently. While the target is unlikely to read them aloud, your brain processes information it thinks about writes, and reads differently than speaking it aloud. The next chapter will look at the exact ways to convey a good work ethic without coming out and saying it.

Brevity is the Essence of Virtue

When something is as simple as a cover letter, that very basicness means every word must shine. While Tolkien became a bestselling author for his pages and pages of lurid descriptions, we must be inspired by Hemmingway's style: short, loaded, and dripping with meaning. While we want to aspire to an almost poetic grasp of the language, we must stop just short of making emotional appeals. Professionalism demands a strict adherence to facts and specifics, feelings and emotions secondary- a close 2nd in the case of a cover letter but bowing to reality nonetheless.

Since editing is usually reductive, the winnowing down process is easier than it sounds. Make sure you have a cover letter you are working on so that as we move forward, you can experiment with various changes as we go along.

Now that your broad strokes are filled in, we can focus on the details.

Break Down

Think about the job you are aiming at. Consider the skills, abilities, and functions you'll require and how your current or recent jobs relate. If you are coming up at a loss, it can help to research what others have done before. Like anything, study the field, your role, and what the company says it entails. Now look at your experience and find all the overlap similarities and stretch to correlation or only if needed.

If you have a lot of words on the same subject, think of boiling them down to essentials and using the space for more supporting facts.

Balance Emotion with Content

Before tabloid journalism infiltrated mainstream news, "journalistic style" would have been too dry to recommend, but so much news content is designed to stir emotions or even tell you how to feel that it might not be out of line. Your cover letter should convey the same wide-eyed enthusiasm as your average high-performing salesperson while remaining professional at all times. In what measure your ratio of passion and information relates to one another will depend on your target. Some companies encourage their employees to have fun and even casual. Others demand a certain amount of formality.

Skills: In or Out

How much job and skill information you include in your cover letter will differ from purpose to purpose. The steeper the change between your experience and your desired position, the more information relevant to your abilities and education you'll want to include. As this may be your first chance to state your case and layout proof of your claim, studying the desired position and any roles it may entail will give you excellent content to address.

Otherwise, if your recent past and would-be future jobs overlap or are congruent enough, you may focus on more specific or personal information. This is where the lesson splits: usually, you do not want to include any negative or pro-active excuses, but if you have no relevant experience, call yourself out but in a positive way, as explained in chapter six.

Overall, make sure you highlight how your achievements and professional experience will enrich the role. Focus on what's unique about you, knowing that the organization will analyze many others beside you.

Mission Statement

Remember that the cover letter is your first and final word about being hired. In a small batch of pre-verified or personally recommended finalists, the cover letter is read first. A cover letter is read last when a tie-breaker is needed, or the resume's contents require further elaboration. Otherwise, they may read it as your interview is being prepared or otherwise to give the hiring person more details.

Your cover letter can tip the scales, so be sure to align everything toward a single objective. It can feel unnatural at first, but once you get into the mode of it, channeling your inner copywriter is easy and fun. Most people going through this guide will have been exposed to so many commercials, ads, and come-ons by the time we are asked to write a cover letter that the style of a pitch or appeal should almost be second nature.

Can You Hear a Smile Through Words?

Stick to definitive, positive language. Superlatives are not out of the question as your goal is establishing your value. Now is not the time for doubt or minor qualifiers: be direct and sure. "Something," "somewhere," and "someone" is to be avoided at all costs. You know what you want and what you bring to the table- it is time to reach out and grab it. Assume the close means not even entertaining the notion of an alternative: you are the best person for this job. All of this, of course, is phrased with positive, even glowing language.

Striking a balance between radiant and obnoxious is a fine art, so be sure you rein it in a little. Writers tend to undersell themselves, but if you are naturally a little bombastic and self-congratulatory, you may want to dial the enthusiasm back a little. Inflated ego and narcissism symptoms *are* red flags prospective interviews look for, so mind you don't stray from confident and into blowhard.

Beyond the Sell

Don't forget to allow yourself room to breathe. While not as crucial as selling yourself and being positive, you want to let a little of your personality in there too. Of course, your unique style will undoubtedly come through; taking some minor liberties with phrasing and word choice can also make you stand out in a crowded field. Mostly this is a matter of not editing your body content too much is takes away your voice as a writer; it could also mean injecting some flavor if you tend to write dry.

Regional terms, industry slang, and popular usage are all generally acceptable, imprinting a person behind the words. Again, formal and semi-formal business environments may inspire you away from such flair, but in general, you want to give the reader a scene of your humanity without pandering to emotions.

Editing Tips

Avoid repeating the same word twice in the same paragraph and overuse in general across the whole. While sometimes there truly is no other way to say something, you will find all sorts of ways to say the same thing with a bit of practice and even research. You want to mix things up and use synonyms as much as possible. Using a thesaurus is fine as long it is to resolve a 'tip of my tongue' issue or otherwise remind you of common words: too much avoidance of repetition comes across as forced.

It is so easy to read something too many times and lose track of basic rules: the brain gets fatigued easily. Once something becomes familiar, your eye can glaze over mistakes or otherwise read it one way when it actually is another. Temporarily **changing the font, colors and size** tricks the brain into reading something for the first time, so as you go through revisions, make sure at least the final editing pass is in a whole different format.

However, *always remember to change the font, color, and size back to normal* before posting it.

Share the cover letter with a friend in the prospective field or anyone in an office setting, and tell them it is for real. Friends may hold back criticism to spare your feelings, so make sure they know it is for real. If you see the person whose opinion you're soliciting is over-kind, tell them you found a template online and personalized it. Given the power of unconscious bias and social interactions, you may want to pitch your cover letter in impersonal terms just to be safe: people tend to be more critical of ideas from outside their ingroup.

Finally, there are endless **examples of excellent cover letters online**, so reading through extant examples of not only approved but laudable cover letters will give you an insight into what the hiring staff is looking for. Part of researching the company and position should be examples of successful cover letters to that field. You can scarcely have too much research where a dream job is concerned, and while you don't want to overthink it, the more you know, the better your interviews will go.

Chapter 3: Step 3 - Know the Types of Cover Letter

We have focused on the cover letter as it fronts a resume for the most part. This is because, by and large, all of the cover letters you write will be in professional hiring settings, with the only difference being what the letter is trying to get the reader to do. Beyond the inevitable job hunting, you can use a cover letter for networking, referral, prospecting, and value proposition. Really, any place you have a body of content that may benefit from an enticing appeal is the right place for a cover letter. Establishing the would-be target usually means making a new template if you make multiple versions for future use.

Keep your cover letters up-to-date and company-specific as much as possible, and keep using fill-able blanks as we did in chapter one to give each one a personal touch.

Network It

A "networking" cover letter is as open-ended as it gets and is almost like a long-format business card. Applied to professional collections, portfolios, and any collection of your professional handiwork, a networking cover letter is meant to be spread far and wide. This means you are briefer and to the point than before- think of the letter as a cold phone call. While eyes can often read faster than we give the typical telephone solicitor, you have a bit more than a second. Bullet points, subtle but well placed, can be used to highlight, accent, and emphasize your smaller word choice. However, a little rich format goes a long way, so use sparingly.

Focus On Strengths and Stay on Task

This is usually an unsolicited, or at least generic, letter of introduction, professional review, and skill set dossier all at once. While I say 'unsolicited,' there is usually at least an inbox or processing algorithm of some kind, so research and tailor as needed. Even more upbeat and glowing than a resume cover letter, the networking cover letter is sterling and congratulatory; the traveling salesperson of correspondence, the networking cover letter is knocking on doors and begging your attention- a figure of speech, of course: don't beg.

Don't Ask for Specifics

Even if you are angling for a specific job, the networking letter should be open-ended and general. Consider what it might have in common with a social networking profile, specifically a professional one. It will present a unified facade, formal demeanor, and open-ended delivery. If your career is focused, fine, but in general, the point of social networking is to make new connections and meet new people.

Learning about opportunities you never knew existed will not be possible if you put yourself in a box, so keep the network as broad as possible. Also consider the actual origin of 'network,' and imagine yourself as the intersection of two strands on a vast interconnected system at work; abstract but potent- you want to find a place where you can catch the most fish. Leave expectations aside and let the world find a place for you.

Consider Timing

Job fairs, periods of expansion, and growth are all usually posted in some way. See the researching and study section further on for ideas on how to time your message perfectly. Beyond posted changes to their staffing requirements, there are regular ebbs and flows you can watch for. For example, near a college, you can count on turnover of entry to mid-level jobs between semesters, especially autumn, as graduates move on to better things.

Any cover letter coming into an HR or hiring department outside the demands of a posted job opening needs to be addressed as networking or prospecting and kept as broadly defined as possible- you never know when you may be thrown into something that just opened up or recently created.

Prospecting

More targeted than a networking letter, prospecting is easier to hone because it is targeted. Networking is laid out as generally as possible, but prospecting is aimed at a particular job or field. Designed to introduce yourself, list your abilities and discover openings, the prospector is essentially a hybrid between the standard resume and networking cover letters.

Don't waste time; thank them in advance and again at the end.

The email will be a waste of time unless you find the right inbox. A prospector cover letter lets the hiring team know you realize there is nothing available now but would like to be considered for positions in the future. You have to do your research to make sure the message doesn't go immediately into the trash, and sending it to people not connected to the HR department or traditional hiring team might even be a possibility. A friend in the company, the head of your position's department, or another sympathetic set of eyes. The likelihood of getting ignored is high, so lead with a good hook and don't spam everyone in the company.

Inquire

A mineral prospector samples ore from all over before determining where to dig. Your letter can serve the same purpose; inquire about openings, new positions, and any immediate company expansions on the horizon. Just as thankless and possibly fruitless as any gold rusher, your messages may never hit pay dirt. Still, the possibility of hitting the mother lode is too tantalizing an opportunity to ignore. Definitely in the "you miss 100% of the shots not taken" and "doesn't hurt to ask" categories, it's a low risk-high reward situation if ever there was.

Value Proposition

Finding your value proposition as an advertiser pushing a product is in all ways similar to a would-be hired propositioning their desired employer. Another hybrid of two or more cover letter types, the value proposition, is an even more pointed version of the prospector and net-worker cover letters. Once you have determined your value proposition, you can use it through the interview process to answer the "tell me about yourself" or "what will you bring to the company" questions. Indeed, if you have worked on the first sentence of the cover letter as indicated in chapter one, you might already have a value statement.

While the traditional cover letter typically covers what you've done for companies in the past, the value proposition letter discusses what you can do for the targeted company. When looking to the future like this, your content can be more hypothetical, as you are projecting what you would do instead of focusing on your past achievements. You still need to use your experience, but it is vital to make sure the desired role fits.

When to Use

Suppose the hiring criteria do not request a cover letter specifically. In that case, you are responding to a massive hiring drive or campaign, or otherwise, when you know the screener will be seeing a lot of cover letters in a short time, go for a short and sweet value proposition. Too small a space to account for much, this type of message is short and sweet.

Short

While the typical cover letter is about one typed page after paragraph breaks and spacing, a value proposition letter should only be about 150 or so words; a single paragraph or two, so short they are more like bullet points.

References Available Upon Request

The "referral" cover letter is written for someone else, personal or professional contact, and is only ever supplied by request: do not supply a personal referral unless requested. Just as the "references" section of a resume has dwindled to the point of obsolesce, you should be wary of supplying personal references unless explicitly asked. A phone number and email address usually provide professional references all the information they need to verify the information.

The first time I ever filled out a job application, I got help from my family. Dad scoffed and said, "that only means you have three friends who'll lie for you," It is also true, while that is a cynical take.

Like a resume cover letter, the referral letter should focus on the good, relevant information, entirely skipping any gaps or shortcomings you are aware of. Consider the reader: make sure you understand the purpose of the letter, but usually it is new hires, so focus on professional traits and skills.

Safety First

The primary reason we don't want to list our references without being asked is related to the reason we liberally sprinkle keywords from the job posting throughout a resume cover letter. The same kind of automated sorting software a job might use to pre-screen applications and resumes can be used by unscrupulous users to scour the web for unsecured names and phone numbers for scams or even fraud.

Front End Content

When you deconstruct what a cover letter of any kind is, it's an attention-grabbing appeal, an advertisement for the self. Not simply putting yourself out there but waving your arms around and hawking like a carny busker. You are both ad and pitchman, selling yourself to the highest bidder. While you can certainly apply some of these lessons to correspondence in general, the whole point of the cover letter as we are working on it is persuasion and enticement. Every bit of the dressed-up department store window display, your cover letter needs to showcase what's inside and make the viewer want to investigate further.

Directed Pitch

Even the reasonably open-ended networking letter aims to get you a job you love in a field you can thrive in. Always make sure the words you choose and the way you phrase things are pointed back at you or how great you would be at the would-be career. Keep that thesaurus handy, look up synonyms for overused words, not overused by you but society at large. While you want to use industry terms, you don't want to bore them.

Short Emails

More and more, our messages are sent electronically, meaning via email. While the subject line and part of the body of a job search email are usually proscribed, that does leave the main body of an email to you. There are a few lines, no more, but an excellent place to position a hook, quick shout out, or otherwise begin planting your seed. Given this is a new frontier of content, there's nothing really expected here as far as format or exception, but readers are used to seeing something here, so make it count.

Sometimes called a "non-cover letter cover letter," this section can be anything we have discussed above and beyond. The best of your attention grabbers, most potent of ice-breakers, or most outstanding possible contribution, this area commands attention without being significant. You may think of it as wrapping paper or gift box: keep it on topic, related but don't be afraid to wax a little casual.

Chapter 4: Step 4 - Find Out More About the Job

Like everything else in life, you can improve your chances of success ten-fold by researching, investigating, and interviewing as much as you can to get started: look up the role as posted and exceptions of other folks who've been in that position. Look at the past and future of your role and keep it in mind as you write and interview. Research company atmosphere, who key staff is, the owner and if the organization is independent and who ones it if not. Learn how to speak their language so you can meet them on their own terms.

At the higher levels of business, consider buying enough shares of stock of a prospective company to get the shareholder report. Publicly traded enterprises are cagey with the public but obliged toward more candor toward stockholders. If it means you hang around the commercial business nearby during lunch and chat up employees, so be it: all's fair, and love and war and chasing down a dream job can feel very much like a flirtatious skirmish.

Know Your Role

The job invariably has a posting, and unless the hiring team is completely losing it, they will have posted the duties and responsibilities of the open position. Not only do you want to know what they *tell* you the job is, but by doing a little investigating, you can find out what the *expected* job will entail. Look out for the old-and-switch when a company posts one position but then tries to hustle you into another; usually, only the tactic of sales, such press-ganging, can be used to fill customer service, seasonal, or other undesirable jobs.

Look up the professional words, research the substitution terms, and act accordingly. The number of synonyms for "sales" is almost beyond count, so if something doesn't immediately come back as a real thing, chances are it's a company looking at "clever" ways to drive people to their sales team.

Stick to Your Guns

Following your dream means not letting someone tell you what it is. Positioning your cover letter to archive one thing and being offered another is fine as long as it's in a related field *and* the organization knows (and is reminded on performance reviews) that you desire a different position. Your research should let you know if the post is related or not. "Marketing specialist" *could* be a job related to advertising and demographic analysis, or it might be the hiring team's way of enticing new people to their sales force.

If your job description says one thing, and the responsibilities handed to you grow beyond that, you begin talking about raises and changes in title. If this happens during an interview, make sure the pay they are offering is consummated with the altered role. Whether by design or poor planning, one job can bleed into another, someone with multitasking abilities is discovered and exploited, or you are otherwise worked more than expected. Know your worth, state your case, and if your value exceeds your compensation, put in two weeks and walk; the number of raises that get denied, then approved after the person puts in their two weeks is staggering.

Learn from the Experience of Others

Make sure to seek out other people's stories with your title and what they do for their job. Just like "restaurant host" has expectations beyond seating guests and general knowledge, every role you might assume in a company is going to have related jobs and secondary responsibility, which necessity or tradition dictate you do. Pay attention to those minor tasks, as they can be a source of experience or irritation. Job needs aren't the only reason you seek out the stories of those who've gone before you.

You can get a feel for the work environment itself this way: the personality of the business is going to be based on the mood of the employees far more than any slogan or mission statement. While it is true that the disgruntled and over-emotional are more likely to leave a negative review than not, as long as you approach your search with the same grain of salt (or a whole salt block) that you do the rest of the internet, you should be able to get a fair idea of how positive a setting it is.

Trends and Patterns

You may discover the company you wish to apply to has been the subject of multiple lawsuits, is predominated by one-star ratings, or otherwise presents as terrible. Even if the organization is solid, it may be part of a threatened job market.

Now may not be the time to buy a semi and a class A driver's license, as self-driving cars are on the horizon and passing you on the freeway. Don't let fear of automation keep you out of the job market, but be aware of what the workforce is doing. In the case of a trucker looking at the bleak prospect of robotic replacement, finding an off-ramp sooner than later is going to pay off. Since the AI Revolution is sure to kill more jobs than just shipping, it wouldn't hurt any of us to think about how future-proof our jobs are.

Programming of almost any kind is always in demand, with infosec (information security) and application development the standouts. Engineers and accountants of all types (actuary came up again and again) make a great living and are seemingly always needed. Every area is different, and if you live in an isolated area, you are going to be limited to remote work or light industry.

Make some of your job searches keywords your city and state, then remote, from home, and startup. The scams and bad ideas outnumber the legitimate offers to an alarming degree, so vet any prospects thoroughly before you even reach out.

Multifunction Letters

A resume cover letter can quickly become a prospecting, networking, or value-proposing cover letter with only a few changes. Take a look at the cover letter you are working on and consider how you can open the ends, expand the reach and otherwise make it apply as widely as possible. We tend to pigeonhole ourselves in life itself. When it comes to profession, many of us not only develop tunnel vision but consciously specialize, never looking outside our area of expertise and into other fields.

Part of your research may have uncovered related fields. Posts from angry ex-employees might be full of heat, but where did they end up? What did they parlay their skill-set into? It can be telling if the majority of naysayers wound in the same field or not: maybe the job itself is awful and the workplace simply average. Use non-definitive and general terms on one and see where it can take you; know that it will be passed over if you make it *too* generic.

Know Your Target

While I have my doubts about wartime metaphors, gathering as much intelligence before your initial sally makes good sense. Social media has made every company an entity you can explore. Even without pushing key personnel through Google, the businesses' own website and links can give you a lot of information. Typically, larger companies have a little bio on some of the public faces, at least going in visual familiarity.

Suppose you know the name of the person who will be reading the cover letters. In that case, it is not sneaky or cyber-stalking to find their LinkedIn or other professional, public website and see if you edit your letter even further. Looking for them on a social site is not advised, as nothing you might find about the individual's personal life would be relevant to the job in question. Beyond the creep factor and lack of professionalism, you wind up in the classic dilemma of the snoop: finding actionable information but being unable to use it without hinting at your betrayal of trust.

Drill Down

There are owners within owners these days, and knowing how many bosses you'll actually have is sometimes a matter of identifying who owns who. While all's fair in love and war, you might not want to accidentally find yourself working for a defense contractor if it is against your ethics. While vegans and pacifists both get used to researching as a matter of habit, one's prospective employers can sometimes get ignored.

The bottom of the website is usually copyright information, and unless the nested business is exceptionally shady, disclosure of ownership is pretty much compulsory. Will it matter in the long run if

ABC Co owns XYZ, Inc.? Well, that's precisely what you are attempting to discover.

Keep It on Task

Ultimately, no matter what you discover about the other party, anything you include in your cover letter must be on point. If their professional, publicly available profile says they went to your same school, let the content your cover letter fronts carry that info; playing up those kinds of coincidences is better as a surprise discovery on their part or casual mention during an interview, or they may believe that's all you have.

Taking the lesson from chapter two, make sure every sentence serves your goal. Take what you learned about the person or group and filter it against your skills and the role's responsibilities. Tangents and unrelated traits are anathemas, a fancy word for a kills-all; The reader's time is a precious commodity, and you owe it to yourself to steward it carefully. Just like a salesperson will wheel any given conversation back to their sale, you must construct every sentence to align with either your past's alignment with their position or their position's fit to your talents.

Know Yourself

After you have discovered the ins and outs of the role, a bit of the company environment, and the projected future of the field, you might get cold feet. Make sure backing out and choosing another field all together is based on a fair analysis of your abilities and temperament, not your brain rationalizing adherence to the status quo. Cognitive bias is the brain's attempt at conserving energy: it will find patterns, make assumptions, and group things into categories, whether true or not. We do what has worked in the past, instead of taking chances on failure, often to the point of breakdown.

Do it as long as the fear itself is greater than the result of failure.

Chapter 5: Step 5 - Polish the Over-all Style

Chapter two gave us style advice you can log for any occasion, while in this section, we focus on content unique to the cover letter. The content was split up because the cover letter is a combination of sales, personal statement, and persuasive essay all rolled into one. The tips and strategies particular to conveying your aptitude for a position are seldom applied outside professional settings. After all, the needs of a job hunter are rarely the needs of the employed.

You are a unique commodity; there is no one who can do what you do the way you do it. You are also friendly, if not approachable, and self-assured but not arrogant; one of a kind but not weird. Unless you like weird, then you're the king of the bizarre. This isn't to mean you're everything to everyone but capable of positioning yourself as top-shelf, premium talent. Convey those uncommon parts of yourself if you can. Keep your content enlightening, though, and never confusing. Stay on topic, cut the fat, wrap it up creatively and *always* ask for a reply.

Always Upbeat

Keep a smile in your writing. When I was working in a call center, they said to speak with a smile on your face: you can *hear* a smile over a phone call. While you don't literally have to grin while typing it out, make sure you keep positive verbiage and an optimistic tone. Balancing an upbeat delivery against sounding chirpy or insincere is the knack here, but having been inundated by advertisements for most of our lives, most of us are ready to mimic the glowing praise used to sell things; this time, however, the "thing" is you!

The tone we are looking for is not ecstatic or even joyful, but the feeling that everything is going to go your way because it always goes your way. Sound ineffable? Well, it's not nearly as intangible as it sounds, and with a bit of practice, you'll be capable of coming across as just the right combination of confident and happy.

Why?

We exude positivity onto the page for many reasons. First and foremost: people like surrounding themselves with happiness. Emotions are contagious to a certain degree, and even folks unaffected by the feelings of others know you are easier to work with when in a positive mood. There's a little cognitive bias involved here, as there is a noted tendency to equate happiness with competence, as the mind jumps to the conclusion that the person is happy for a reason.

There is a repellent quality to desperation. Most of it is unconscious as the mind distances itself from unwanted feelings. We do the same thing with depression: the discomfort of being reminded of life's misery is dark enough to turn away from. This is one of those penetrating lessons that strikes our experience's core. "When you laugh, the world laughs with you; when you cry, you cry alone" is a truism for a reason.

Confident, Not Arrogant

Another trait that's easy to overcompensate for and slip into its negative extreme, confidence, is a powerful, sought-after trait, while arrogance turns people around in their tracks. While it may seem like a razor-thin margin between the two, once you understand the difference, you'll see that it's not a slide-bar like happy to ecstatic, but two peaks of distant mountains.

Confidence is capable but knows the limit of their expertise; confidence says "I don't know" as readily as "I know." The confident person admits mistakes but learns from them. An arrogant person is slow to assume blame and seldom admits to the holes in their education, and repeats mistakes for all their claims of infallibility. The hallmark of arrogance is condescension, and while talking down to people is hard to do in correspondence, it is possible to go overboard in building yourself up.

Confident prose isn't boastful but factual; staying on topic and not offering unrelated traits and experience keeps you on track. If you are concerned about coming across as over-qualified, you leave stuff off. A braggart announces their great skill; the confident simply do it. In the case of a cover letter, it means you state you are the best person for the job and use the rest of the body to emphasize why, connecting everything to the role.

Why?

Many of us have it ingrained in our heads that admitting any errors is a sign of weakness. Another famous mental pitfall is letting one's expertise in one subject lead you to think you're an expert in all of them. Nobody wants someone on the team to think they know it all, if not for the apparent social chaffing, but in a professional setting, you have to be ready to set aside how you do something and learn a new way. Of course, sometimes you have a more efficient way of doing something, but if you've been browbeating and mean-spirited, no one will listen. Again, this is the cache attached to bravado and arrogance- most of that won't come across in a cover letter.

A Note on Admitting Error

We have already excised any negativity or pre-emptive explanations (see also: excuses) from your cover letter and made sure the resume is on point as far as relevancy and accuracy. When it comes time for the interview and the job itself, be sure to watch and listen for a culture of personal responsibility. Sometimes, the environment is so competitive that nobody admits to mistakes, so the only person owning up to missteps appears to be the one making errors! No one is right all the time, but no one is wrong all the time either.

Good Weird Not *Weird* Weird

The line between wonderfully eccentric and unpleasantly strange differs from person to person and even from day to day, or hour to hour. Professionally, there is going to be a company line on the topic, if it differs from 'business formal' or business casual.' Even within the realm of company policies, you are going to have room for the expression of personality.

Hobbies should be left off unless they relate to the needs of the position or company spirit. Same with civic or social clubs, unique talents, and unrelated certifications or awards. The exemption to "stay on task" is if the pastime or accolade requires a high degree of precision, follow-through, or teamwork. There are universally desirable traits almost every employer looks for, and if you can find a way to include rock climbing (for example), it will speak to your resolve and dedication- it takes training and bravery to assail a cliff face, and most employers realize that.

Universally Desirable Skills

Universally desired skills include:

- Teamwork and collaboration; accurate language, effective delegation, and receptivity
- Math and numbers; programming, accounting, or management
- Multitasking; effective project juggling and laser-like focus

- Ability to learn and relearn; take instruction, adapt, and self-instruct
- Office computer knowledge; hotkeys, and basic Microsoft Office software
- Communication skills; polite, professional, and factual

If your resume doesn't reflect any of those, find a way to include them in your cover letter. There are more and still other skills particular to your desired field, so make a few keyword searches and find the far-out, unusual, or unique needs of your target role finds desirable.

Paintball or airsoft ranges are great places to learn teamwork and group coordination, but unless the person is personally familiar with the sport, they won't understand the dynamics involved in that kind of group play. Briefly list or bullet point the relevant skills you use if you choose to include them. Typically, the harder it is to explain, the more it needs to use a desirable skill-set. The reader's attention is a precious commodity, and while owning a dozen aquariums and terrariums requires a good deal of organization and dedication, it may not be the best aspect to showcase.

You Do You

As a lover of all things strange and unusual, you have to learn how to rein those darker and more provocative aspects of yourself in a little. Specific skills and traits tick the boxes but are socially repellent or at least avoided. By the time you're to the point in your life where you're writing cover letters, chances are pretty good you have a handle on what to broadcast and what to diminish. Let your freak flag fly in your personal life; at work, we have to be a little more discrete; pin a tasteful freak flag on your lapel if you don't keep it at home altogether. I cannot be any more specific because what is considered an "outsider" will differ significantly by region and office.

When in doubt, opt for reserved. Streamlining, reducing, and summarizing means leaving anything questionable aside anyway, so take a second look at company culture and revise.

Less Is More

The cover letter should be straight to the point more than almost any type of correspondence you can write. While you shouldn't have more than a single set of bullet points, presenting short bursts of data like that is what you are looking for. Use keywords from the job description to seed the text; mentally switch places with a harried, overworked application screener and consider what they would expect, love, and hate to see. Consistently perform to your audience, anticipate and adapt, but constantly be winnowing away, pruning, and reducing.

While sometimes "more is more," in the case of expressing your fit for a position, if you could use symbols and icons, we would, but any graphics should be limited to color splashes or rich text. Minimalism shows sound design principles and showcases the content, however, so unless your desired position values creativity or personal expression, think twice about even tasteful embellishments.

Don't Dream It: Be It

"Fake it 'till you make it" works as long as you can manage at least a little bit. Learning hotkeys and navigating standard office software will ensure you don't have to be taught to walk before your run; hit the ground running by taking some professional development classes or familiarizing yourself with the expectations of a modern office environment. Everyone has to start somewhere, and now is the time for you to start the next stage of your journey.

Chapter 6: Step 6 - What to Avoid

Like anything you might create, the cover letter has traditions and styles you dare not betray, as well as red flags and common mistakes someone screening the inbox will be triggered by. While editing should be a foregone conclusion, overworking a piece can make us blind to

errors. Even after using the hard edit tricks, you can fall into the trap of wanting to include too much. Of course, the medium creates the environment overuse the certain words is nearly unavoidable, but repetition is usually the death of interest. Make sure you never mention other applications, point out your shortcomings, leave obvious questions unanswered, or talk money.

While you feel like "getting out in front" of the compensation, the only possible sticking points you want to volunteer on a cover letter are gaps in work history and holes in your education. Holes include skills and experience, as more and more jobs are OK with a certification or proven track record if not degree or job history. If the void is minor enough, you may just want to ignore it. In fact, once you have put all the positive and relevant together, there is little room left. On the other hand, if there is a glaring defect or shortfall, there is a chance it's not the deal-breaker you think it is.

Ignore the Elephant in the Room

What you are agonizing over might not even be on the radar of your hiring person. You might be making a mountain out of a molehill, and the questionable item is of minor concern to them. The offending article might even be a fairly major flaw, but they have decided to overlook it for whatever reason. Or they *have* overlooked it entirely, and it may one day cause you problems- but not today. In almost all cases, omitting, gloss over, or diminishing the negative is a good idea.

Don't throw yourself under the bus, shine a spotlight on flaws, or otherwise suggest reason not to pick you. Because of the previously mentioned lack of space, the cover letter and resume can both lack your serious shortcomings. Let them come up in the interview or during orientation. If you discover something you thought was a flex-point is unbendable, speak up. Employers love to hype a remote position then ask for hours in the office once you're interested. Perspective employees love to say they can do something but can't.

Know your needs and understand the full scope of your prospective roles' responsibilities before you attempt to skip over a significant problem.

Don't Overwork It

You bought a guide on perfecting the cover letter, and if you took my advice, it's an open document on your desktop or at least near at hand. If you haven't noticed, a good idea that gets taken too far goes bad; those with enough experience in the arts know how you can ruin a masterpiece by not declaring a stopping point. After a certain point, you must be finished; countless editorial passes might be desirable for a poem, work of fiction, or emotional autobiography, but when it comes to the cover letter, you must know when to say when.

Keep fiddling with the vocabulary, and you run the risk of the cover letter sounding canned, forced, or otherwise disingenuous. In the spirit of 'less is more,' recognize that there is a stopping point, and in the case of professional correspondence, it's about three passes: rough draft, working draft, and final draft. The working draft is for fiddling, rephrasing, and reworking; it is where we are now. A final draft should be printed out and read via hard copy and the dreaded "red pen of doom" brandished. While non-writers may not live in fear of the editor's mark, the editing process is reductive, and nobody likes the sound of your voice like you do.

With the danger of agonizing over every little detail is acknowledged, let's look at some of the not-so-minor details that trip up the best of us.

Repetition Repetition Repetition

In your single-minded approach to landing your dream job, make sure you're not using the same terms again and again. We have already talked about using a thesaurus and internet searches to find suitable synonyms, but there are other words or phrases which crop up even when those precautions are taken. Also, whenever you reach for an external source, be it thesaurus, dictionary, or other resources, make sure the new material stays within your style, vocabulary, and professionalism.

Avoid overuse of the word "I." While unavoidable (nobody is saying "don't say I"), you want to avoid it in general. When writing anything autobiographical, the most common word to overuse is I. Look at places where the second and third 'I' in a sentence can be removed, letting context give the sentence its subject. Don't go to such elaborate lengths as to make a cumbersome, unnatural flow, but be mindful of the overall cadence and structure in any case.

Beyond replacing "I, I, I…," make sure the key terms we asked for and included did not become laborious. You want to make sure the reader knows you are on point as far skills go, but once it becomes apparent, we're repeating ourselves on purpose, the positive esteem flips and becomes bland pandering. They know what they're looking for, and once they see that you have it, you won't need to beat the fact over their heads.

Facts Are Facts

We don't want to bore them with echoing rhetoric, but we can't cut repetition at the expense of accuracy. Specialized knowledge, subject matter experts, and high-level degrees all require a tremendous amount of overlap in skills and job history, so don't shy away from proof of your mastery.

Your One and Only

While it may seem like a lie of omission, do not mention any other resumes you may have sent out. In advertising, we call it "building urgency" or "establishing scarcity," but in a job market, it tells the recruiter that you have options on the table, they are not your first choice, or you are not 100% invested in working there. There's not a hiring team out there who is going to assume you are only applying to one place. If it's true, the cover letter should establish the target organization's exclusive status, though you then have to rush to explain why.

No Numbers

The cover letter is not the place to discuss pay. Time enough for that in an interview, and your previous salary is similarly something you should not provide until requested. Some places put their pay rate front and center. Others will wait until they know what you expect to be paid before saying anything. There is wisdom in doing so, and leaving that information for them to provide is always a good idea: you never know when their standard rate is higher but stick you at a lower point because that's what you asked for. Similarly, the organization might be paying below industry norms, and have you employed before it's discovered.

Chapter 7: Step 7 - Special Cases

Every rule has an exception, for there are no absolutes. While we've beaten the 'no negatives' drum loud enough, sometimes a red flag waves so boldly there is no ignoring it. When life or choice has created one or more problems, you are encouraged to get in front of it. While plenty of issues may require direct confrontation, no work experience, no opening posted, over-qualified, and parenthood should all bear a mention. Parenthood shouldn't be a problem, but if the aforementioned research yields a good-old-boys culture, you may want to diminish or leave it off if you attempt to join them.

Usually, the majority of non-standard cover letters come from the game-changers: job transitions, prospectors, or value propositions. These letters are a shot in the dark, the boldest of bold moves- unsolicited and unexpected, your messaging has to be tight, your delivery brisk *and* engaging, and it must be timed or aimed correctly.

Lack of Relevant Skill

Probably the primary reason a resume gets kicked is a lack of experience with the posted role. It can seem like a catch 22: you need job history to land the job in the first place. While it can seem true, if it IS true, then you will find schools and courses teaching it. Investing, Real Estate, and even law in one state doesn't require a license but has so many laws, loopholes, and work-around that *not* getting a certification or degree would be like joining the Major Leagues as an amateur. You may not completely fail, but the learning curve is likely to hit you like a wall. Still, personal background or self-education, just plain-old passion and tenacity, can take you far. We all have to start somewhere, so if you do not see any side-doors, start searching for the entry-level position you want.

Computer Network Administrator could start as a Desktop Support person, and while rare, there are examples of CEOs rising from the lowest ranks of whatever company they now run.

Come Clean

Do not spin unrelated skills or fabricate abilities if the trait is required for the job. You can fluff passing familiarity up into competence and competent into skilled, but taking a zero to a ten will get fired, and if the community is small enough, possibly black-listed. There can be a flame as long as there's an ember, so analyze your background and keep adding to a running list if you need to. Following your bliss is just another way of saying do what makes you happy; hopefully, you'll have had enough interest in your past jobs to find even a shred of relevant knowledge to apply to a dream job.

Don't just get in front of your ignorance but blast it from the first line. "I want to start the next stage of my life, and XYZ Industries can take me there" communicates your desire and sets the stage for the reader to expect some shortcomings in the resume. Think of ways to highlight the positive side of a negative situation. You're not leaving a job you hate but seeking better opportunities, taking an enterprising sabbatical, and looking to better yourself. Make the new job a part of your evolution, not a stop-gap to get food on the table.

Dream Job & Workplace

Maybe your research has turned up not only a position that requires those skills you love to use but has an environment just as perfect. Just like some people you can meet and feel like you've known for ages, there are some workplaces which just click. Prospecting and value props are all fine and well, but when it comes to attempting to woo the company of your fancy, you can be so pointed as to draw blood. Dramatic similes aside, if your target is specific down to the physical location, you should aim that cover letter right for the heart.

Go over their mission statement, study the website and corporate structure. Peruse their social media, business to business media, reviews, testimonials, and anything else so get an idea of their vocabulary and overall vibe. I am sorry for using such an intangible term like 'vibe,' but no matter the size, purpose, and leadership goals, every organization has a feel, an emotional undercurrent that is all-pervasive.

Timing Is Everything

All of these investigations should turn up a job fair, peak season, or other opportune time to send your letter. If it is indeed a cold call, out of the blue, appropriate of nothing, be sure to acknowledge the timing; but consider asking about upcoming openings or projected growth and try again then, because asking someone to 'remember me for future openings' is unreliable. Even if they loved you, time diminishes everything, and things get lost, so ask for a possible timeline and keep them on your radar.

If the company uses a staffing agency or website to source talent, create an email alert for them so you can track openings and company news.

Sometimes "no" is "not right now," too, so be sure you reply to places you really want to work.

Over-Qualified

The ability to simply omit higher education or skill mastery is definitely tempting, though the people who take a severe dip in pay grade seldom stay at the lower echelons for long. As suggested, explore the underlying tasks in the field you are looking in so you can at least entertain your fancy in a more meaningful way.

Mainly, the employer will be worried your dramatic career change is temporary, and you be leaving them for greener pastures as soon as you wise up. The cover letter is a great place to express both sides of the issue- not only how much you want to do what they are doing and why, but also how crushing the career you are getting out of. People understand job satisfaction and, after the tribulations of the pandemic and the social unrest it stirred up, one's personal happiness, and more importantly, not hating your job, is paramount to most of us.

Is There a Future in It?

An excellent way to cement the idea that you're not going to fly by night is by expressing an interest in the field as a new career. A former Wallstreet broker who wants to landscape could just as quickly say they are interested in starting a landscaping company as not; true or not, it gives you a reason for being there that is more understandable than sunshine, fresh-cut grass, and physical labor.

Parenthood

Never diminish or omit your family to get a job. If an organization truly does not respect the hard work and mental discipline it takes to raise children, it is doubtful that any amount of bullet points or descriptions of your workload will sway them. Emergencies, school breaks, and other requirements will make themselves known in due time, so hiding them is usually a fool's errand.

Own it. Little else in life is as universally understood as being a parent, so brandish your stewardship of young lives with the same pride you would like a Ph.D. or Key to the City.

There is also some "you probably wouldn't want to be friends with someone like that, anyway" mentality here, too: an employer that would denigrate the tremendous responsibility of raising the next generation is probably going to have other toxic work culture elements, too.

All of which emphasizes the points outlined in the first chapters: go for it! You will be surprised by the advances you can make once you get into the habit of trying. Don't talk yourself out of putting your resume and variations of the cover letter into places you consider a long shot. Very much in the spirit of "aim for the moon; so even if you miss, you'll end up among the stars" philosophy, you must keep trying if unsuccessful. Victory only goes to the ones who stay in the race.

Conclusion

As much as I have avoided personal anecdotes in this guide, my experience transitioning from retail to sales, then into a 'new customer welcome team' then 'account manager' perfectly illustrates the power of a good cover letter. What happened to me goes on to present a few of the core concepts earlier, not least of which is to carefully word things to be open and inclusive. I kept getting lured back to sales because it is the "always in demand" field I was part of for a while but got out of as soon as possible.

I was stuck in retail hell; nothing but "cashier and light stocking" as far back as high school, where 'car wash attendant' and 'grocery store bagger' were left in obsolescence. As a means of getting away from the liquor store I was working at, I took a job as a "vacuum technician" or "cleaning equipment marketer" of some such "clever" euphemism for door-to-door vacuum cleaner salesman. It was difficult, with long hours and a degree of manipulation and high pressure I hated. It did, however, account for three months of my life and was not standing in front of a cash register.

As much as I hated the job, it went on my resume. Only a quick sentence about direct sales near the end as I was applying for something, anything, which would pay better than minimum and get me off the street. Literally on the streets- my sales crew made weekend road trips to nearby cities because they had already worked a lot of areas close to the office. When I found a customer service call-center job, I jumped at it. Not an out-sourced, temp, or a remote phone bank, we were working in the same office as everyone else, which is excellent for working your way up.

They saw my door-to-door experience and wanted to put me on their sales team, pointing out just how hard knocking doors is. I insisted I didn't want to be in a selling position. It turns out they understood and asked because, in a few places, the cover letter stated how eager I was to take on new responsibilities, learn new skills, and otherwise get out from under my job history. There was a position on the 'new accounts team' that had a sales-like element (saving cancelers from dropping the service) but was overall what I was looking for: customer service, with an eye toward eventual tech support or IT.

Had I not included those terrible weeks hawking vacuums, I never would have been considered for the better-paying position of sales, or what they considered a related post, new customer orientation. Had my cover letter not expressed enthusiasm for the company itself, skills and experience related to computer fluency and their business, and an eagerness to join in any position they thought I might thrive in, I may have been stuck in customer service first, if not passed over entirely.

So take up your pen (I know it's likely a keyboard), make a few drafts, and nail the delivery. When you get the interview, make sure your cover letter isn't the only thing you studied upon. Nailing an interview can be intimidating, but with some foresight and more research, you'll be on the staff in no time!

Book 2: How to Write a Resume

7 Easy Steps to Master Resume Writing, Curriculum Vitae Design, Resume Templates & CV Writing

Theodore Kingsley

Introduction

Welcome to How to Write a Resume. There is nothing more exciting than the prospect of starting a job you actually want. So many of us get into the habit of taking the first available position and settling in that we forget to try and find a career we actually like. The whole idea of Follow Your Bliss can seem like an empty platitude but if you really want to live a happy life, then dreading the workweek is not the way to do it. When you find a job that speaks to you, which ignites your passion or at least draws your interest, knowing how to put together an excellent resume can mean the difference between getting an interview and winding up in the recycle bin.

After we look at the bare necessities, all the possible items and add-ons are gone over, making sure nothing they ask for catches you by surprise. We analyze the usual format resumes take and how you can use eye flow to bury or highlight information. Knowing when to Fake It till You Make It starts at the resume, and without a clear set of rules, you can find yourself in a real jam. There's nothing like actual professional development, however, and you'll also find crucial office and lifestyle lessons that are fast or crucial to pick up.

Design and layout are explored, the fairly rigid standards used in resume creation are fortunately diversified by alternative formats, giving the would-be hired plenty of options to showcase exactly what they want. While interviews are another topic entirely, there are a few simple things you can always keep in mind once your resume is selected.

Finally, it is always good to keep in mind the danger signs a business might provide a poor work environment. Learn to recognize the red flags as you interview the company right back. After all, if you found a job that seems too good to be true, there is a chance it just might be.

Don't let yourself get tripped up when you're trying to climb the ladder- whether it's the traditional corporate ladder or the creation of new opportunists you make for yourself, get a handle on your introduction by making it as strong as possible.

Let's get started!

Chapter 1: Step 1 - Master Resume Basics

While there are many formats you can use to layout all your information, the content itself is almost always universal. Some examples are given later on, but for now, let's make sure you have the essential data straight. The resume is your appeal, supporting argument, and summation all at once; the resume speaks for you and is often the only contact you will have. Regrettably, many times a resume is declined. A wide talent pool, specific requirements, or gaps in your skills or work years can all cause you to wind up in the rejected pile.

So let's get your ducks in a row and make sure you have the best chance possible of getting a callback.

What a Resume Needs

At its most elementary, the resume gives the employer everything they need to choose candidates for an interview. They work as an introduction and statement of intent; some employers read them first and give them tremendous weight. Others never even look at them. Your name and contact information are a given, but remember to add an email and even relevant social medial URLs; Professional sites like LinkedIn, MeetUp, or AngelList all strive to create formal networks between business-minded folks. Relevant work experience and skills give the company an idea of your abilities, schooling, certifications, and applicable official recognition.

Contact Info

Your name, where you live, and contact information go at the very top in nearly all the resume layouts I've seen.

Make sure the phone is your personal number; never use a work line.

The address should only include city, state, and zip, not the house/apartment numbers. Unfortunately, some discrimination based on where you live is possible, and if you are from a zip code with a bad reputation, feel free to use a family or friends. Then when the "error" is discovered, ideally, you will already have proven the bias wrong once you make the "correction." Accuracy is crucial, so *at least* using a residence you can receive mail at is recommended.

Email address is typically required, so make sure yours is professional or at least work-appropriate. Make a new one if you created the old one with an unprofessional name.

Modern resumes contain a web address, too. Making and maintaining a professional web address is good practice, with LinkedIn specifically being called for in many web forms. Details on curating a positive and professional digital footprint are gone into later on. Still, at its most general, you have either A) never post anything you would not want your boss or clients to see or B) keep a separate social media account for biz. Whatever you do, make sure the URL is as short as possible.

Headline

After your contact info comes the resume's most eye-catching feature: One sentence to hook them; try to limit this to about ten words. Placed at the top, just like regular headlines, it serves as a super abbreviated pitch or clickbait-style interest generator. *Always* tailor this custom for the job being applied to, including keywords from the posting and job title itself. Use title case (Capitalize The First Letter Of Each Word), **bold** or a Slightly Larger font to make it stand out from the rest of the resume.

Once you get a keyword or two from the job posting and the title you're seeking, that only leaves a few words. Go for a strong, definitive tone; avoid imprecise and casual language. Definitely no slang or expletives *unless* the company positions itself that way; even in the case of edgy or "hip" company personae, do a little research before you go throwing informal language into your one and only header.

However, if you are not making a dramatic change, you might not want to populate this area at all. It is a waste of breath unless you have something to say which isn't noted in your work history.

Work History

Under the headline should go the bulk of your resume: work history. This section will be short when you are young or have been fortunate enough to work for the same place for an extended period. In general, resumes only want the last three jobs you held. The fine art of resume targeting is gone over in detail later on, but in short, never feel like you have to include *everything*. If you hated a job or are making a career change, you may just want to leave some things off. Still, if it is a big chunk of time, include the work experience anyway, though you must be ready to actively resist getting pulled back in. Sales, in particular, are always sought after and hard to escape once you get into.

Keeping a list of your past employers, the period you worked there, and up-to-date contact info for them is always a good idea. Best case scenario, you have the direct line to someone who was in a position above you, knew you personally, and will sound happy to hear your name.

What a past employer can tell a reference check differs from state to state, so if you get fired or know a negative review lingers behind you, it might be a good idea to leave it out altogether. If you fear the worst and must include a business you know you offended, sometimes it is best to enter the contact information for HR or even a main number, not your direct supervisor.

Do Not Include References

Unless specifically directed to do so, do not include references at all. In those cases, make sure you tell the person you are listing them as a reference so they will be expecting a call.

Objective or Summary of Qualifications?

Some people may choose to include a brief list or bullet points showcasing their relevant skills between the headline and your work history. You are generally discouraged from adding this to resumes unless you are doing a career change or don't have a lot of job experience; skip this step if you are in the same role. Career counselors rarely recommend this information, so unless you meet the circumstances mentioned earlier, it is recommended you leave this off entirely.

Perfect Everything

Now that all your information is collected, organized, and at least roughly where you want it on the page, you have to go through it and make sure everything is not only spelled right but up-to-date. Not only contact info that actually goes where it should, but inclusive of recent changes, too.

Spelling, Syntax, and Resume Traditions

You can use abbreviations to save room, but they must be business-standard. Absolutely no emoji or text/social media shorthand. A quick web search for Standard Abbreviations will give you an idea of what you can use, though don't overuse them; too many abbreviations are not only hard to read but unprofessional.

Eye-flow & Format

Take advantage of the way we naturally read things by placing things you want the reader to look at the top left and items you wish to diminish on the bottom left. We also tend to scan in a clockwise pattern when we're not reading; both go from left to right, and while adhering to the layout expectations, you can play around with key placement a little bit.

Consistent

Make sure dates match up. Your work history is going to have a location, so double-check that it corresponds with reality. Keep all your contact info channeled to professional destinations, and if you have a provocative or controversial lifestyle, I am sure I need not remind you to keep them untangled.

Make sure that you use the same shortened spelling in every instance if you abbreviate anything.

Cover Letter

The cover letter is important enough that it could be an entire book unto itself. Organizations of all kinds will often request a cover letter, so knowing how to address non-profits and academic institutions can be helpful, too. Sticking to just business professional, you want a cover letter to be condensed, with little to no personal fluff; as always: weigh best practices against what you know about company culture.

While not every job source will read every cover letter, the cover letter can easily be the tiebreaker if an employer is deliberating between two candidates.

A chance to state your case if changing careers or coming back to work from a period of unemployment; see Padding later on if you have gaps more significant than a month or two.

Short & To the Point

The cover letter is your opportunity to sell yourself, position your resume as the standout and otherwise get your first and last word in.

Like the headline, include specific call-outs to the job description and title. You want to position yourself in the best possible light, so make sure every word is on point. The information you might have added in the "objective or summary" area goes here: skills, abilities, and *related* experience. Always Be Closing and urge the entice the reader to read your resume.

Chapter 2: Step 2 - Know When to Use a Curriculum Vitae

A curriculum vitae, often abbreviated CV and Latin for Course of Life is a short-written synopsis of your professional life. These will be requested by name, so do not include a CV unless one is asked for. Include work experiences and skills, usually related to the desired position, though they are usually quite thorough. Affiliations, honors, awards, and any kind of official recognition should be included, too. While a CV and resume are not the same things, the confusion between the two has caused some organizations to refer to any short CV as a resume.

How It Differs from A Resume

The size and depth of information in a CV mean it can be many pages long. Try to keep it to two pages, though academics and upper management maybe longer. Depending on your profession and lifestyle, it could very well be many pages long! Not just work experience but any sort of civic or commercial recognition or accolade. You can also include published work; in short, anything you have accomplished that few have, or which was recognized by an official body.

In general, you find requests for a CV in academia, investing, science, and any profession that might benefit from someone of diverse skills and interests. Again, nobody will care if you were a junior varsity track and field champion unless the job is a physical trainer or in some way related- keep content directed toward your goal at all times. Sometimes you will have to enter an unrelated entry to account for the time; even then, since a CV allows for a few words describing the activity, you have a chance to bring the reader's attention to related facets they may not have considered. Don't stretch credibility, so make sure your allusions make sense.

What Goes In

Keep the content professional. It does not have to be directly related to the position you are applying for; it just has to paint a complete picture. In the case of changes in your field, be sure you highlight the steps you've taken to learn new skills.

Do Not Include

Never give too much detail: as counter to the idea of delivering your complete history as it seems, it is best to be brief. Your audience is reading dozens, maybe hundreds of these things per hiring; Just the facts, relevant tasks, and time frame, then move on. Never bury the lead- put the relevant part front and center even if it's not in the standard order.

You are not obliged to include every little thing, especially if it does not serve your plans. It has been said repeatedly: *it is OK to omit jobs you don't want to go back into*. Even if it means rephrasing your job title, you are allowed to bend things a little bit to make them fit. Precisely what to bend and how far before it breaks will depend on the skill and is gone further in the Padding chapter later on. Far from duplicitous, padding is a time-honored tradition, walking a fine line between making things up and stretching the truth.

Overqualification

If you desire a job at a lower level of pay, the operation will (rightfully) be afraid of you leaving for better money elsewhere. Do you want to feed fish at the city aquarium? You might want to leave off your history of managing million-dollar portfolios; on the other hand, why not consider a snorkeling instructor or research assistant? "Slumming it" may be lower stress, but your previous positions will open doors for you that would be closed for others.

Personal Information

No personal information is included- that's what the resume is for. Beyond your name and contact details, do not waste time trying to elicit sympathy, familiarity, or appeal to their emotions. There is a time and a place for that- this is your stat block if you're a video game character or your dossier if you're a government asset.

Do not call attention to flaws or shortcomings by preemptively explaining them. An excuse in any form is unprofessional. You **supply explanations if requested** but avoid making excuses in almost all cases. Low test scores, lack of transportation, and handicaps that will not affect your ability to do your job should all be left out. Let them ask; volunteer nothing.

Volunteer and Intern Positions

I see conflicting advice on **whether or not to include volunteer and intern positions** at all. Of course, if the work you did relates to your target job, by all means, add it. For the most part, however, they should be left off altogether- unless they apply in a meaningful way to the desired job or account for more than a few months. Setting up a free food kitchen for the needy would be left off unless the job you are applying for is related to food service or helping the needy. Falling under the general advice of not playing on people's emotions, many will see such inclusion as grandstanding or self-serving *unless* the position you are applying for can relate somehow.

Irrelevant Work

Bad or irrelevant work histories you can leave behind you. Don't even include it. If it means gaps, you might pad the area with anything you did during that time that relates to your target profession. In the CV, **unlike a resume, gaps are usually preferable to fluff or unrelated work**. Gaps can be spun and otherwise accounted for; your stint as a singing messenger won't help you get that accounting job, though, so just leave it off.

As I said earlier, by **law,** some states can only confirm your dates of employment; others are a bit freer with **what is allowed to be disclosed**. A quick web search will give you a short answer, as that kind of information is seldom posted in the workplace but frequently asked (and answered!) on public forums across the net. It is always a good idea to work and leave under the best possible terms anyway. Legal requirements aside, most fields are smaller than you think, and there is no telling when you will run into an old boss again.

Education & Certifications

Education should be included, with grades and dates, and as summarized an overview as possible. Early in your career, your educational background will be a more significant selling point than later.

Finally, any **awards or certifications** you have achieved should be tucked in near the bottom. Relevant to the desired position, hard to win and otherwise given by a large or respected group should be your rule of thumb. If you are applying to be an accountant, your plaque declaring you January's Best Bagger at the grocery story store you worked at could be left off as irrelevant. On the other hand, if you were given the Presidential Medal of Freedom, it might not apply to be a bean counter, but you may just want to mention it.

Layout & Format

It pays to use less information in a larger font size with more blank space in order to make things easier to read; most employers are going to be looking at piles of these things, so while you need to be thorough, you must weigh that against brevity and ease of reading.

Name and contact details go on top.

Under your name and how to get ahold of you is the "**personal profile**." One used to write a short personal statement or mission here; however, it is pretty apparent the intent; you want the job, so a brief professional summary can go here now. Snappy and encapsulating as much as possible, quickly state your career skills and goals in about five lines or so. Do not stray, stay on topic, and remember your audience: a busy HR representative or your would-be boss if it is a smaller outfit. Just like the resume's obsolete "objective" area, a mission statement type message here will work if you are changing careers or otherwise taking a shot at a position you have no experience with.

The bulk of the CV goes under that: **core competencies, experience, education, and skills**. Under as mentioned, any hobbies or interests you include must be on topic. The " key skills " or core competencies area is the section between work history and personal profile is the "key skills," or core competencies area. Make this a showcase of abilities and traits ideally suited for the job. This is a cherry-picked, buffed to a shiny array of the exact skills you'd need to perform the job in question. Take advantage of keywords. In a digital format, this will trigger searches, and with a human reader, it will pop off the page if they are scanning. We have repeated and rephrased it so often I might as well shine another light on it: use words from the job description and title to highlight your matches.

List everything in *reverse chronological order*- start with your most recent and list backward.

Make sure your history accounts for as complete, unbroken timeline as possible. Any gaps should be accounted for as professionally as possible. Taking a month off to drink on a beach doesn't sound as good a "took a restorative retreat" or even the catch-all "personal reasons."

Positioning, Targeting, and Professionalism

Given the range of items you can include on a CV, you have a lot of room to position yourself in the best possible light. Emphasize those jobs and skills which apply directly to your desired position. Take everything you want to minimize at the end or leave it out altogether. This is your customized info drop: you have the opportunity to compile, edit and omit your history until almost every element underscores your strengths.

While you will definitely want to make up your curriculum vitae and keep a basic model on hand, taking even a few minutes to selectively add keywords and specific elements for each use makes sure it's on point.

You may even want to leave some words or phrases as blank, (____), or [content] so you remember to customize each one. Again, this isn't you inventing things or stretching your grasp past your reach; spin, position, and reminding people of a trait's applicability is what you want.

For instance, "line cook" is fine if the people processing your application know the ins and outs of food service. Still, you could add a few points to drive the workload home: "short-order chef regularly processed 100+ orders per hour with over 99% accuracy" paints the picture vividly. In the same way, "customer service" tells you nothing, but "agent with a 30 call per hour average and the highest quality analysis score three months in a row" gives the reader the whole story.

Even if your position was relatively sedate or straightforward, find the glory (or at least the high points) and highlight that. If moving between fields, your challenge is finding the similarities, overlapping skills, and otherwise agreeable traits between the two jobs and making that your focus.

Chapter 3: Step 3 - Pick & Choose Your Presentation

Putting everything we have learned so far together, your objective should guide your content. The key to good writing, in any form, is to remove anything that doesn't move the plot forward. Even in a resume, this holds true. Pare down, streamline and condense. Another general rule of content production is targeting your audience.

We take it for granted that you will be using professional, polite language throughout, but you should also keep in mind the size of the business and the workload of the hiring team. Even if it's a small group, everyone appreciates a writer who respects the reader's time. Just like the best of journalistic delivery, stick to the five Ws and little else.

Skip the bad stuff, gloss over the poor and spin the unavoidable. This is not only your best foot forward but a step in the right direction, too.

Make It Your Best

As mentioned earlier, you do not need to be thorough at the expense of your credibility. Since the layout is reverse chronological, the farther back in your history it is, the less you are obliged to add it. If you took a job just to make ends meet and have no desire to persuade any of its elements, skip it entirely or keep the entry as brief as possible. Focus on the desired and dwell on the hopeful.

Look at the suggestions later on or make a quick internet search for "resume templates" or "samples," then choose the layout which best highlights your skills as they relate to your objective.

If you are already working in the field, your best bet is the usual-standard resume formats highlight one's present job. Forms that bring skills or education to the fore should be used if you've been training or have gone to school for your desired position.

Only Include Your Desired History and Skill Sets

Positioning yourself in the most favorable light means knowing the job description *and* its unstated roles, too. Any job posting will have bullet-points and an explanation, but you should go beyond what the company lists and research what other people in that exact title have performed. You might find overlap to your existing abilities, or at least start thinking about how you'll respond if it comes up.

Strategize and Plan for the Interview

Research the organization you are applying to. If another company owns it, look them up. How formal is the work environment? What types of staff does it seem like the place employs?

I have discovered errors the interviewer thanked me for, red flags I required an explanation of, and even court reports or employee complaints which made me look elsewhere. You probably research big purchases, but so few people spend any time looking into a company they are about to join. you can find a more complete list of red flags later on.

After you have placed only the most targeted information in the resume as possible, the interview should be steered in your favor as a matter of course. Having focused on your correlation to your chosen career, the interviewer refers back to the information provided, they're being reminded of your aptitude.

Identify Weak Spots

Mind any gaps in your professional history and be ready to account for them. Do not explain unless prompted, and make sure you have something at least personally enriching prepared to say. Be ready to abridge or skip that year you spent in a kitchen when you're applying for a clerical position. Most places just want to know you were doing *something,* and if it means inventing something unverifiable to avoid an unfair reaction on their end, so be it. Employers are most concerned when you spend a long time looking for work but not being picked up for anything.

"Job Hopping" is another thing a screener might look for. While there are resume formats that you can use to diminish this unfavorable trait, just like someone looking for a monogamous partner, any would-be employer is going to be extra wary of someone who changes jobs every six months.

An inconsistent career path will also raise a few eyebrows, past a certain age, of course. A checkered experience list leaves you looking spread too thin with no deep knowledge or staying power; job-hopping is generally frowned upon.

Plan for Damage Control

Make some internet searches for "common interview questions" and begins thinking of ways to answer them. If you have weak spots, this goes double- know that it might be called to your attention and have a ready reason. Avoid blaming others or circumstances; take personal responsibility by stating what you learned or how you will avoid such problems in the future.

As long as you do not repeat a mistake, you can always think of a misstep as a learning opportunity and move past it. Employers like to think in the same way, and most will look past a few minor flaws as long as the whole is strong.

Life Skills & Personal Experience

As we have stated, make sure everything is aligned with your goal again and again. When the resume or CV calls for skills and any non-job-related experiences, it is an invitation to present those aspects of yourself which may not otherwise get a chance to stand out.

When to Include

We have talked about what to include but made little mention of nonobvious things you can add. Once you've made a list of your achievements, awards, and official recognition, think about the skillsets used *and the skills people assume you need.* Something like "janitorial" might seem like a stop-gap you want to gloss over, but if you so much as changed a light bulb, you can name that role "facilities." If you had a checklist that you were required by law to complete (OSHA or other standard bodies), rename your position "compliance."

A quick internet search should yield some options beyond the norm. This is one way you can pivot from one field to another; the career change is not as dramatic once you find some alignment points. However, do not stretch past credibility and always stick to established synonyms. From the earlier example, if all you did was clean, you don't want to risk looking disingenuous (big word for a little lie) in the eyes of a new boss. If your current role is an endless uni-task, look for new skills to pick up that might be useful in your future.

On the other hand, getting tasked with jobs that are not part of your job description can be frustrating in the extreme because they are usually not compensated. Someone hired for "customer service" might find themselves performing stop-gap IT services if the individual knows computers. The rule of thumb is that if your new jobs take up more than a week, you should ask for added pay.

While you can "lie by omission" without fear of deception if enough time has gone by, critical points on the resume simply cannot be bent or stretched. Of course, all the contact and statement-style sections, but your recent work history must be as solid as possible.

Be Thorough in Recent Past

As poor as anecdotal evidence is, when I made my first career transition early in life, I made use of a skill set I had thought I wanted nothing to do with. By the end of my post-high school/during college, my retail career (grocery bagger, cashier, etc.) had moved across the country and found myself as a door-to-door vacuum salesperson. For three or four miserable months, I sold (or attempted to sell) heinously expensive home cleaning machines to random houses, and there was not a single facet of that job I enjoyed.

It was too long a time to gloss over, *and* I was attempting to transition from retail to office environments. With a good deal of trepidation, I entered Direct Sales in my job history but applied to everything that wasn't sales-related. Sure enough, when it came to the interview, they asked if I would be interested in their sales team- I said it earlier. It is an axiom (a universal, unchanging law): salespeople are always in demand everywhere. I had had enough of Getting From No To Yes, so I had to restate my desire to get out of sales and into virtually *anything* else. I wound up in a position with an almost sales-like component: new member orientation. While it had what I was looking for, interacting with people, teaching, and information services, I had did have a specific retention rate I had to maintain, which was essentially re-selling someone on something they wanted to return!

Ultimately, you never know where a company might place you as long as you are open for different positions during an interview. In the last example, I had gone in to apply for a basic customer service role, but, seeing my sales experience (everyone knows how hard door-to-door is), they let me know about a job in the new members' team which *they hadn't even posted yet*. Had I left off the sales experience, I may not have had the opportunity to start at the better-paying position.

Digital or Hardcopy

Make sure you have both a digital version and physical printouts of your resume when you go into an interview. It may never come up and go unneeded, but having copies of your resume on hand is like carrying an umbrella: it is better to have it and not need it than need it and not have it. There are quite a few symbolic "umbrellas" which are universal in professional spheres, the most relevant to your resume I included later on.

Having both a link or draft email with a resume attached ready in your inbox and a few printouts of the resume on hand will make sure you are prepared for anything. While you may not have the opportunity to use them, if there is more than one interviewer, making sure, they each it in front of them will help them focus on your credentials.

Do Your Homework

Make sure you read and re-read everything they send you and the original posting, too. Go one step beyond and read up on the company: their web page, of course, but relevant links off that, too. It can give you such an inside track on your interview and the questions you ask when it is your turn that I am saying it again: research any organization you wish to be part of. You will not only know how best to phrase your resume and, if requested, CV but give you a firm understanding of the situation you are walking into. Asking questions of your interviewer once they ask if you have any is great, but asking intelligent questions is even better.

Once you know everything you need to about the organization you are trying to join, you will know exactly what they want to hear. If your resume is not looking up to the challenge, there are quite a few things you can do to bend, twist and stretch the truth without breaking it.

Chapter 4: Step 4 - Know When to Pad

It is controversial and, yes, not exactly the most evenhanded approach you can take, but sometimes the "fake it 'till you make it" approach is the only way forward. There are also occasions when the job posting contains prerequisites far beyond what the role actually calls for. This may result from a hiring director making errors in what the position calls for, or it may be a red flag that the company wants to use you. Sometimes you won't know which is which without getting a foot in the door.

In most cases, you are only nudging your career in a better direction, exaggerating, adding spin, or "padding" what is *already there*. We all know exaggerating, in this case, taking something you did once or rarely and making it out to be a more significant part of your role than it was. Dodgy, sure, but not a lie. Spin is rephrasing one job to sound like another, again not deceiving outright but repositioning or reinventing.

Fake It *Only* If You'll Make It

People have been fired, even sued, or jailed for inventing false credentials. Don't worry. If it ever comes to legal action, it will only be you having knowingly put the company or lives in jeopardy: don't do that. It is called "padding," not "fabrication." It is the fine art of making a molehill into a mountain or calling a swamp a wetland in more practical terms. You may not always be able to pad something out, or perhaps your new position is too far removed from the last. Still, there's no harm in letting your reach exceed your grasp ever-so-slightly.

Bending but not breaking the truth sometimes is the practical side of "dare to dream" and "shoot for the moon." Our strategy assumes you have at least a novice-level idea of what you are doing because unless you luck out and get placed with an excruciatingly patient co-worker, few places are going to want to pay for your training if said training is part of the requirements. Have you ever been that unlucky sop who's stuck between "ratting out" an ignorant co-coworker and just giving them a little on-the-job training?

I don't mind showing someone hotkeys or how to use Task Manager, but if the job requires basic PC use and they're asking you how to copy and paste, it's going to be a bast first few months. Hint: there *are way* too many tutorials and how-to's on office desktop environments, not to at least shoot these floundering friends a link or two.

Dangers of Deception
Even if you manage to smooth things over or otherwise have proven yourself by the time the truth is revealed, your co-workers may

not appreciate their hard work and dedication being skipped by some up-start. Even if the truth remains hidden or you are fired, the most pressing danger is winding up in over your head. Any job is going to be stressful enough without adding the necessity of learning not only on the sly but on the fly. Any organization needs you to be a link in a chain of activity, usually more like a tangled, interconnected web than a chain, but *that* metaphor is taken. The point is that most positions in any business will be connected to more than two others; the better-paying jobs usually come with more responsibility, which generally translates into even more points of interdependence. Being the weakest link in a situation where you are more like a hub than a spoke can be disastrous.

If it means you take a lower-paying position in a related field, sometimes that is what you need to do. Night classes, internships, and volunteering are all good opportunists to build skills you may not have had a chance to practice.

Learning on the Fly

Do you have the skills but lack the credentials? While some careers absolutely will not let you in the door without the proper certifications (be it levels of schooling or trade licensing), there are plenty of very well respected and high paying careers with low points of entry. In the best-case scenario, you can go home after orientation and cram, study yourself silly, and otherwise take a crash course.

Some jobs will throw you into service on day one, but there is at least a day of orientation and welcome in most cases.

It is dubious in the extreme, and as cautionary as I am, the possible benefits and rewards are just too high. In the risk-reward balance sheet of life, saying "yes I can" when you really mean "I think I can" is right up there with approaching the people you're attracted to and conquering fear on the list of crucial life skills. Always remain open to new ways to present your professional self, too.

At one point, when I was jobless, I picked up a short-term gig moving office equipment out of and into shipping containers for the expansion and remodeling of sizable office space. As we set up all the new workstations, I made it known that I knew computers (Hey, should I hook this desktop up? Let me know if you see an Ethernet cable!"). While I had a PC at home, it was for gaming, not office work- at that point, it was not even online! I had to lean on my landlord for weeks to get the jack fixed when I finally did. But because of the mystique surrounding computers and my general comfort looking stuff up, I was hired as a temp on their IT team for desktop support. They knew I didn't know how to network an intranet or even add new members to that intra-office system, but I knew enough to get started.

From entry-level desktop support to server management, most computer stuff only requires expertise. Even coding software is more "prove it" than "where'd you do to school." Desktop IT Support doesn't even require too much in-depth technical ability, just practical knowledge of what's what and how to Google it. However once you put Information Technology into a job title, people get all kinds of funny ideas. Due to the world's reliance on computers, any job is going to take a second and re-consider someone with cyber-skills— more on this and more career fuel later on.

Flaws Into Benefits

Do not be so fast to undercut yourself. Good advice for life, but it is even more important on your resume and CV. I talked earlier about not letting gaps or unrelated skills into your pitch, but let's look at the idea of positioning something in a new light as it relates to things you might want to leave off altogether.

The *only* long periods or abilities you don't want to include are ones that make you appear unprofessional.

Those odd jobs you held can be bundled together into a single category or group and called "seeking my passion" or "career exploration." It's a whole bunch of dead-end jobs. I don't think the world will hold it against you if you say you were busy working on yourself; if your young, this isn't even an issue- many of us spend our early years bouncing from place to place, living for the night and weekend.

Never let "homemaker" make you feel inferior: that is *hard work,* and if you don't know how to phrase the duties required of someone raising a child or children while trying to maintain a household, here's a jumping-off point. The information given next is also a rough guide on breaking something off-base down and finding its business applications.

I made a quick list and got cooking, cleaning & picking up, running errands, and taking care of children. I would feel OK about listing that on a resume, but you could rephrase some, if not all, of it for someone who has not actively raised children.

- Self-motivated
- Meal Planning
- Managing Dynamic, Inexperienced Team
- Multitasking
- Maintain A Clean and Safe Environment
- Driver and Personal Shopper
- Emotional Support and Empathetic Communication
- Calm Under Pressure

There is a significant number of women employed in HR positions, so hopefully, you'll be screened and interviewed by someone at least sympathetic to the role.

Homemaker is just one of the most accessible examples. Make a list of the skills you performed at any job, especially those you were less than thrilled with. This break down of tasks is handy when the job was recent or too long to omit or gave you skills you would like to use again. Again, most employers just want to make sure you weren't passed out on a park bench somewhere. Which isn't to denigrate folks who've been homeless so much as to remind you many employers will.

Spin vs. Ownership

It can be difficult knowing when to hold something back and when to add it. There is something to be said for the personal strength required to kick an addiction, overcome homelessness and otherwise improve your situation. America loves to laud the underdog, celebrate people who overcome adversity, and "pull themselves up by the bootstraps." The ironic thing about the "bootstraps" phrase is the full quote is "NOBODY pulls themselves up by the bootstraps," it is from the Army and refers to everyone pulling each other up and working as a unit. The fact that it has come to mean the opposite is frightening enough to make you want to leave some things off.

Research, research, research. You will find companies founded by people who have been through what you've been through or are savvy enough not to hold it against you. You will also find companies that tout some kind of ethos or assumed moral high-ground that would exclude you; better discover it before you even step foot in the door than week two.

Chapter 5: Step 5 - Add to Your Resume

Knowing what feathers to stick in your cap can be daunting. If your resume is weak or you are looking to give yourself an edge, having some auxiliary education *and* the certification to prove it can mean the difference between landing in the "yes" pile or the circular file (office trash cans are often circular and no file is). Old dogs can learn new tricks if the treat is right, and they try it a few times. Given the term "dawg" has been in use for a few generations now, that is not even a metaphor!

Don't let the idea of learning something new stop you. Find the basic, entry-level form of whatever you want to learn and start there. Just like lofty career goals you might not reach, you will wind up with something close or headed in the right direction.

Continued Professional Development

At its most basic, you have to look at what will benefit your chosen career the most. One of the few catch-all skills you learn is desktop computer environments. Most business is done on PC and design on Apple, though that is less true and more of a generality as time goes on.

Towns of almost any size have basic computer skills classes you can take. Libraries, community centers, and adult education institutions of all kinds host "introduction to PC use" style classes as well. Do not pay more than a modest amount, if at all, because YouTube and other platforms carry free how-to content of anything you can imagine. While some of us benefit from having a teacher, you can learn a surprising amount by seeking out tutorials.

Do Not Discount Skills Learned from Current and Past Jobs

Some of us middle-aged folks have accumulated quite the curriculum vitae behind ourselves, and while we don't need to be complete, we should never forget to include relevant details. Even young people with little to no job history can plumb their past and find a marketable skill or two. Mowing lawns can easily transition into landscaping or horticulture, or any kind. All those late nights you worked at a dinner in college taught you stamina and a 'can do' attitude if not congeniality, food prep, or basic logistics.

When you bundle a group of unrelated jobs, either unrelated to each other or your target job, make sure you're not throwing the good out with the bad.

Resume Fuel: Universal Abilities *Every* Employer Desires

While every position is going to be unique, there are quite a few things that carry over to so many places it may as well be universal. Like a musician learning musical scale or an athlete working on cardio, you should have a basic grasp of the following, if not a working knowledge.

- *Communication*

Fundamental to any office job is the ability to get a message from one point to another. Written, spoken, or otherwise telegraphed, you must know how to email, address envelopes, carry on a professional conversation, and express yourself with a minimum of personal information and elaboration. English learners are encouraged to practice often anyway, though seeking to climb professional ladders should find a club, group, or any kind of gathering to learn from.

- *Filing and Bookkeeping*

Simply keeping an organized workspace on the casual end, the specific job of handling spreadsheets, managing official documents, and maintaining the company ledger is its own thing. An official bookkeeper tracks transactions, debits, and credits are recorded and transcribed. Producing financial statements and other crucial reports makes this career detail-oriented. At its most basic, learn a little bit of Excel or at least how to navigate it.

- *Typing*

Practice typing if you know it's going to be something you will be doing a lot of. Just like how your muscle memory will kick in when playing a video game and pretty soon you don't have to look at the controller, not looking at the keys while typing is developed over time and with repetition. Studies prove that occasionally glancing down or back and forth doesn't slow people down as once believed.

- *Basic PC Use*

As stated before, the only thing holding you back from learning how to be a basic computer user is you. Tell yourself you *can* because, at this point, computers, their peripherals, and most software are so user-friendly your grandma could use them. Between knowledgeable friends and family, free videos and classes, and just opening menus and exploring the system, you can learn quite a bit.

- *Customer Service/Interpersonal Communication*

Customer service and interoffice talk should both be carried out in dignified, professional tones. Unlike customer service, you seldom need to force congeniality in an office environment, but you always must remain calm. Stick with need-to-know when dealing with supervisors or during work sessions, and if your naturally intense or show emotion easily, try to carry yourself with a bit of dispassion. Formal business environments aside, even the loose, casual workplaces require you interact with each other in respectful tones.

Microsoft Office

We have already name-dropped Excel, but the whole suite of Microsoft Office products will probably come into play sooner or later. Their word processing program Word is universal to the point that other competing products mirror their layout and even terminology. Same with all their Office applications; any spreadsheet software that *doesn't* lay itself out like Excel is going to find itself fighting an uphill battle. PowerPoint, Publisher, and to a lesser degree, Outlook and Access all adhere to and set the standards of user interface and functionality. There are free versions to learn on and even use instead of Open Office and Office Libre. You can download those for free, and they nicely mimic the licensed stuff.

Google

The little search engine that grew into a colossal corporation offers a few sought-after certifications; though they might not be in your wheelhouse, it is good to know what they are, not least of which because they affect the average consumer. Google Analytics is the flow of people in and out of your website, how they got there, and what they did. While this info is pretty easy to get, knowing what to do with data and what it represents on a deeper level is a powerful tool to have. Same Google Ad certification: once a paid service, the steps to get Google Ad Certified are now free. Knowing the ins and outs of search engine optimization (abbreviated SEO) is a benefit to customers and businesses alike.

Personal Traits

Few endeavors will have as far-reaching effects on the quality of your life as taking personal development seriously. While professional growth will carry you far, personal growth spills over into professional and takes you even further. Ignore fads and office trends, and stick to time-honored traits which have withstood the test of time.

- ### *Self-Motivation*

One can quite literally base an entire career on motivating people. The search for willpower and the ability to stick it out are in such high demand you can rest easy if you only show up on time, do what's expected of you, and do so consistently. If there is any personal development that overlaps not only work but also your personal life, it is motivation. Do it as soon as you think it. Procrastination is the death of enterprise.

- ### *Research and Self-Education*

Look stuff up, don't accept "I don't know," and stay curious. I've heard it said, "it's so hard to know what to believe in this day and age." While there is a whole lot of half-true and just plain lies out there, anyone who had to write a paper using cited sources or can read the bottom of a web page and look up the publisher can quickly parse fact from fiction.

- *Reflection*

Think about the past; consider your effect on the people around you. Learn from your mistakes and occasionally look backward. Hindsight is 20/20, but so many people are blind to it because they never take the time to look at their lives and accept responsibility for their actions. Don't self-flagellate, however, and blame yourself for too much.

- *Emotional Intelligence*

Profoundly crucial in your personal life and almost as crucial in your professional space, emotional intelligence knows how to deal with feelings and those of others. I should say it's "ideally" less critical in a business environment because we should be setting our emotions aside and focusing on the task at hand in a professional setting. In reality, we are human, and even the best of us takes out frustration on our fellows. Mind your thought-action-emotion cycle, and don't let personal turmoil cause interpersonal problems.

Remedial

We all learn differently, and seeking to fill holes in your education doesn't mean you are dumb- quite the contrary. Acknowledging your weaknesses *and taking steps to address them* means you are at least aware of what you *don't* know. Self-awareness and self-improvement put your head and shoulders above most of the population, no matter your skill level.

It might have been decades since you went through school, or maybe some things were always a little difficult for you. Whatever the case, there are tons of options for people looking to continue or refresh their education.

Math

Without the website Khan Academy, I would have been unable to pass college math; all levels from basic to calc are covered, walking through equations and talking out the process. It is free and used all over the world. Khan also offers courses in most major subjects, from Chemistry to History.

English

To this day, I still rely on the spell check built into my word processing software, as well as the website Grammarly for fine-tuning. Not perfect, AI and algorithmic grammar checkers are still prone to error, so be sure not to simply approve every suggestion without reading it.

Reading something out loud can also give you an idea of it is written clearly or not.

English learners are encouraged to double-check necessary forms with a native speaker just to be sure.

MS Office

Learn the ins and outs of the Microsoft operating system (Windows), as well as MS Office and the related apps your job might use. Like I said before, look for freeware parallels (OpenOffice, LibreOffice) to practice and learn before paying full price for the package. There is always the possibility your worksite has a way to get you a copy of Office or pay your subscription to Office online, too.

Other Skills

Your research into the prospective position should yield a set of abilities people in that role should have. If you find any gaps, usually a quick web search for "tutorial," "introduction," or "how to" will give you the insight you need to begin practicing.

If you require some specialized equipment, libraries have far more than books to borrow or use these days, and so-called 'maker spaces' fill in other gaps as well. Look around, ask around and do more web searches- if your favored career is obscure, you may not find public places to get your hands on it, but clubs and even enthusiastic individuals all love

Chapter 6: Step 6 - Dodge Resume Red Flags

While we've glanced over some danger signs and deal breakers employers are triggered by, we never took a probing look at how to deal with issues in your past, or at least problems with "how you look on paper." At the same time, you should be looking for red flags of your own. While times are tough, you should know the corporate equivalent of an apparent scam or slipshod operation.

Mind the Gaps

Having looked at the importance of accounting for yourself for any period greater than a few weeks, let's look at avoiding those altogether, as well as identifying why they exist in the first place. You may find that there's no reason to gloss over or invent an excuse once you look at what was happening at that time.

Typically, we can't function without a job, so the personal motivation to be constantly employed is somewhat built into American life. Take a look at *why* you have significant gaps in your timeline. If you are just picky and were looking for work that whole time, were you living off savings or depending on someone else? While you may have thought of it as draining your savings, you can phrase it more positively: having managed your money with such efficiency, you allowed yourself the luxury of being picky when transitioning. By the same token, you can admit to being "fortunate enough to have a partner willing to support my dreams" or something similar.

We have already defined how to list the super-powers that come along with parenthood. Nannying, even just babysitting, is not something to leave off if you're still young and the scale of your services was large enough. Everyone probably helped watch a younger niece or cousin at some point but if you have a group of neighbors and family friends who called on you routinely, entrusting you with children is a mark of responsibility if nothing else.

Reflect, deconstruct, and translate the tasks to biz-speak, and you should be on your way.

Match History to Target Job

Sporadic or tangentially related job history is one thing. But walking into a place with no experience in even a related field is seldom going to work. Unless the placement is entry-level, you'll need *something* to get your foot in the door. Having looked at what to do to patch holes in your education earlier, there's less to say here, save a reminder to be extremely wary of taking just any job because you're in a pinch.

Should you find yourself in a bind and need to accept a position that you *know* is temporary, you owe it to yourself to keep looking once money is coming in and not fall into complacency in a role you hate. Most employers won't take you on if they know it is going to be short-term, so it might be a good idea to remain cagey with that information. On the other hand, staffing agencies are how organizations find temps and seldom offer permanent positions. Instead of wasting time and resources of a company hiring, training, and entering you into their system only to have you turn around and quit, besides temp services, the modern gig economy is more robust than ever, and more jobs are job types are added every day.

Digital Footprint Awareness

Many employees have been brought low by their personal life overflowing into their workspace. Doing a basic internet search on a prospective employee is not as common as you think it is, though you must always carry yourself with the knowledge that anything you post anywhere is just a few clicks away. As that sort of lesson is relatively endemic to our age, you should watch out for more easily overlooked digital pitfalls, too.

Outdated Professional Sites are still there, whether it's the LinkedIn profile you never updated from five years ago or some long-forgotten social start-up that never actually faded away. Google, Bing, and otherwise internet search yourself and all the spellings of your name which you've used now and then to make sure.

More likely is **embarrassing or inflammatory content** coming up in interviews or reviews. The usual Facebook or Instagram party blunders are bad enough, but many public records and news stories are online. Our online selves don't die until the company hosting the content does, and even then, the data is likely to live on in the new company's possession. Even if you delete it or the organization goes bust, an internet archive like The Wayback Machine takes 'snapshots' of the net every day and can usually find even removed content. Someone going to such extremes to ferret out information on you would be rare to non-existent, but those kinds of sites are why people say: the internet is forever."

Red Flags on Their End: Interview Them Back

We can get so focused on landing a job or get dazzled by a good front once there that it is possible to let go of good sense or gloss over warning signs. Just like someone lonely and desperate taking a partner they may not even like, desperate times calling for desperate measures can lead you to more trouble than it's worth.

Find the names of the owner or CEO and research them. Do they have a physical address; PO Boxes are common in the professional sector but can be a red flag if there's little other information. The more information you can find on them, the better. Phone numbers, external sources vouching for their legitimacy, and a brick-and-mortar presence are all signs the company is legitimate.

Public Feedback

With the advent of diverse social networks, sites like Glassdoor, Indeed, and LinkedIn all offer employees both disgruntled and enthusiastic about sharing their work experience. Just like product reviews, look for more high ranks than low ones, and know that a few single-star reviews don't mean the place is the pits. Read the reviews, take them with the same grain of salt you do *anything* posted by random internet strangers who are possibly angry. However, the sites before have a higher degree of personal accountability; by and large, you cannot post anonymously because they are also job sources. The fire and vitriol you find on informal sites are largely absent for the most part.

There's nothing quite like asking around, and making small talk about your new job to people can be revealing, too. Sometimes everything on the website, in the interview, and even as far as employee orientation can be staged to come off great, but the underlying work environment still is terrible. Catching people's initial reactions and drilling down when you sense hesitancy can be revealing to the field itself, if not the job site in particular.

What to Ask

At the end of the interview, they *should* ask you if you have any questions. In fact, them *not* asking you if you have any questions is itself a red flag! We wouldn't tolerate a date who went on and on about themselves any more than we should respect an organization that doesn't care about the opinions of its would-be staff.

- The Basics

When they are interviewing you and giving information about the job, listen for the following: what are your day-to-day responsibilities? What are your obligations overall? Are there opportunists are in my role for advancement within the company?

- What's the best part about working for this company?

- Where do you think the company is headed in five years?

Start here; these are almost expected. It's "a gimme" and should loosen up the other side. You can expect a canned or at least a semi-rehearsed answer, as this is the interviewee equivalent of "what do you think your strengths are" and "tell me about areas you need to improve on" on the scale of predictability.

- Why is the position open?

Listen for this to be answered in the interview. Often, it's expansion or the simple creation of a new role. If their answer is evasive or imprecise, you can expect it was either a sudden leave or high turnover, both of which can be worrying. Happy employees give notice, and positive work environments aren't constantly seeking new workers.

- <u>How long have you worked with the company?</u>

Knowing how long the person interviewing you has been with the organization can tell you many things: if the place is worth sticking around for, if they promote from within (most people will tell you if they started in a lower position spontaneously), and usually an idea of how their accent went.

Interview Danger Signs

Many businesses say they are pro-veteran but fail to consider hiring one. It pays to dig deep when you do your "due diligence" and research your would-be employers' owners and their owners if possible. A company can front as much as they want, but a trail of lawsuits, bad press, and new, aggressive or predatory ownership are all hard to hide and definite red flags.

No physical space at all, no phone numbers or email address for the usual public faces an organization presents: president, HR, even just a generic Contact Us page, all indicate a fly-by-night enterprise. Think of how much money most businesses put into marketing and brand recognition; any place leaving those areas empty is leaving money on the table at best, poorly run, or actual criminal activity at worse!

Most business owners are pretty proud of having started a business, and any parent company is going to brand their property. Be as crime-aware as you would be around a new individual: it is perfectly OK to be inquisitive, or even interrogatory, if they are going to be in your life for a while.

Chapter 7: Step 7 - Understand Resume Design

There are a few universal traits any format is going to follow and a wild diversity past that. We will look at a few standards, a few differing and new designs, as well as the names and places you can look for free templates. Like any medium in use by a vast population, "resume" is a living language, its format governed by trends and usage changes just as much as a spoken tongue. Let your grandma teach you recipes and other life lessons, but you may want to take a bit of generational perspective with her resume advice.

We went over the most common resume layout in chapter one, so when we go through the following, be sure you consider the form. A program like MS Publisher will let you drag and click custom text boxes, letting you create a flow you like. Since not everyone enjoys design, there are hundreds of templates and fillable forms you can find free online. Assuming you are taking the "I can do anything" approach, let's look at the content a resume holds and where folks typically expect to see it.

Layout and Format

First off, as we go along, "top" can easily be replaced with "upper left" when talking about the layout of practically anything which is read by audiences who read from left to right. Some languages are read from right to left, and those countries have their own design theories.

I have seen quite a few "modern resume" examples which use a **headshot or graphic embellishments** to add a greater degree of visual appeal. A bold bar, fine line, or soft background color can all be used to add some beauty and dimension. While it may seem overkill and too much eye candy will distract or even lose a screener, a little color or a professional-looking bust may not hurt. If your target job is in any way creative or the company presents a 'fun' or 'hip' face to the public, make an internet search of "modern resume example" or "resume layout template" and take a look.

The resume standard is similar to the curriculum vitae: **your name and contact info** are the first things you see. No matter the layout you choose, your name, and how to get ahold of you, go first. It should go without saying that your name is your professional and/or legal designation, not a nickname. If your nickname is your usual name, putting in quotes between your first and last name is permissible but isn't as professional as simply stating as you meet people.

Same as a CV, you leave the building numbers off your contact info, sticking to city, state, and zip.

Ensure the phone number is entered correctly and never use a work number unless a personal one precedes it, and they are both labeled.

You need an **email address**, and if you don't have one by now, there are literally dozens of highly trusted email providers and hundreds more beyond that. Most are free, and if your existing email has an unprofessional address, it is past time to make a new one and keep it exclusively for professional use. Plenty of larger organizations will provide you with an intra-office email address, so taking the step of making a new one might not even be necessary.

After your name and contact info, a mission statement or some kind of declaration used to go here. Since the resume's goal is inherent to the medium, "hire me," this area is now for **skillset overviews** (if anything) and only hold a **personal statement if you are hoping for a career change** or otherwise have a Need to Know to share with the reader. There's a good chance you may **leave this off entirely** if your position is not changing or the relevant details are included later on. Again, we have to value the time of the hiring staff. If what you might say here is said elsewhere, then save your breath (so to speak).

Work History in reverse chronological order goes next and should comprise the majority of the document. Usually, each job gets its own entry, with dates, locations, and contact info followed by a *brief* description of your role. I can't emphasize enough how short the entry really can be. Most hiring personnel will have a reasonably firm grasp of different jobs and their responsibilities. Be sure you elaborate if the role was unique or was later expanded to include other duties, but if it was pretty standard, rattle off a few of the significant tasks and move on.

Be ready to talk about *any* entry on the resume, especially the most recent.

Templates, Style Guides, and Software Suggestions

I have yet to use a word processing program that *doesn't* offer a Templates option in the File dropdown. Open up templates, click resume and fill it out. While generic and brutally simple, that should be OK for most uses. OK is far from excellent, however.

The more robust the design software, the more template options you are likely to have. Play around and use one which highlights your strengths and diminishes your weakness.

You can always begin shopping around if you feel the extra polish and shine on your resume would be worth it.

Etsy seems to carry a surprising amount of beautiful resume templates, surprising until you remember they are an art and design house first. While they are at cost, there are many stunningly well-done examples.

Make Your Own Template

Looking at a published, or otherwise premium, resume can give you inspiration toward mocking up your own: there are free versions of all the popular layout, publishing, and design programs if you're just babbling or don't want to make the investment.

Anything you write, design, or layout can be turned into a template by simply using the "save as template" option under File→Templates in most menus.

Less Is More

As far as good textual design is concerned, the more you can remove, the tighter and more compact the content, the better. While personal aesthetics may differ, when you are talking about the realm of professional layout and design, minimalism and brevity are the rules of the day. Don't gloss over anything in your bid toward simplistic design but use negative space and a clean, easy-to-follow structure to showcase your abilities.

Conclusion

I hope I have given you everything you need to put your best foot forward, and I wish you the best of luck on your career path. Luck is a funny thing, however, and while we like to think of it as chance and random, there is definitely a lot you can do to tip the scales in your favor.

Your next step is to get this hot new resume into the hands of would-be employers, and beyond the fleeting advice I included about interviews, make sure and do for your face-to-face what you did for your resume: study, review, and revise. Since you cannot practice the interview itself, you can read up on common interview questions and investigate the corporate culture and see how you should dress.

Thank you for trusting me to guide the next stage of your journey!

Book 3: How to Develop Your Career

7 Easy Steps to Master Getting Promoted, Salary Negotiation, Career Development & Acceleration

Theodore Kingsley

Introduction

Welcome to How to Develop Your Career. Are you ready to develop your career further? Or maybe you're just getting started on your career and don't know where to begin. Either way, you are at a very interesting crossroads. You might have experience elsewhere, or you could be starting from scratch. No matter what, however, you will need to know how to develop your career. Just about anyone can learn from being able to work on their career better, and that means that you should be more than willing to do what you can to work on it. If you want to be able to bring yourself that career success that you have always dreamed of, then you are in the right spot, and this guide is going to help you achieve it.

Ultimately, working is something we all must do, and that means we all need a work plan as well. You need some sort of idea of what you want to do with yourself so you can actually succeed in the world. No matter what it is that you will go out and do, you ought to know that you have options. No matter where you go or what you choose to do, if you are able to make it clear to yourself that you are working on something, you should be able to succeed.

Building that career development plan can be done in just a few simple steps—7, in fact, and we are here to guide you through them all. If you are ready to get started, then let's begin—you will find that being able to get it done is going to benefit you significantly. As you go through this guide, you will be guided through 7 steps that will help you to develop your own career. We will begin with defining goals, so you know what you are doing in the first place.

Then, we will take a look at what you can do to identify your own strengths and weaknesses. From there, we will work to establish a game plan. Networking comes after that, followed by taking opportunities that are afforded to us. Step 6 brings us to being accountable for our own actions and recognizing that ultimately, we hold the responsibility here, not anyone else. Finally, step 7 in career development is constantly working to better yourself.

By always striving for better, you put yourself into a perpetual state of development due to the fact that you simply never settle. If you can do this for yourself, you will find that you can develop your career. You can discover that you will actually be quite capable of becoming the person that you want to be.

Let's get started!

Chapter 1: Step 1 - Identifying Your Goals

Before you begin working on developing your career, you need to know what it is that you are setting out to achieve. Do you want to be a CEO? A doctor? Do you simply want to run your own business without having to answer to anyone else? No matter what it is that you want to do, you can figure it out one way or another. You just have to make sure that you set yourself a goal.

Roadmap to Success

Goals are like our roadmaps to success. They help us to get from point A to point B without getting lost. Let's say, for example, you want to become a doctor. Your goal is there—you know that you want that MD as your end goal. However, how do you get there? You would need to go to school. You would need to pass several tests and more. Of course, that all require you to be willing to do so in the first place. By having your goal in front of you, you will begin to see that roadmap plays out in front of you so you can follow it and achieve whatever it was that you set out to do in the first place.

Within this chapter, we are going to establish just how important it is for you to begin identifying your goals so you can utilize them. We will see how they are able to motivate people and ensure that we stay on the right track. We will go over how to set a professional goal and how to track it to ensure that you are on track. Finally, we will go over the importance of maintaining motivation without feeling lost or stuck. This is imperative to this process—if you cannot maintain that motivation, how can you ever possibly achieve those goals that you set out to achieve? This problem keeps people held back—it makes people feel like they don't want to bother or like there is no point in trying.

Why You Need a Goal

Everyone needs a goal. Defining your career goals is one of the primary parts of getting ahead in the professional world. Those longer-term goals are what will push you forward and achieve what it is that you have always wanted. When you are able to achieve that ultimate career through planning, you will realize that it was all worth it, but for now, you will simply have to trust that it will all work out in the end.

We all want to move forward, personally and professionally, and that means that you have to do something about it. If you want to get back on track and ensure that you can succeed, you will need a goal. Have you been stuck in a rut for a while? Are you still caught up in that same job that you've been trying to escape from for a year? Are you stagnant professionally? All of these are signs that you need to set some goals and get your career development skills right back on track. It isn't always easy, but it is important, and it is something that you ought to work hard on to make happen. If you can do this effectively, you will discover that you are much more capable than you probably thought.

When it comes to setting a goal, however, you will need to follow certain steps that will help you to ensure that you are successful. If you want to ensure that your goal will actually be compelling enough to keep you moving forward, you need to feel like you can move forward.

Setting Professional Goals

When it comes to setting professional goals, you will need to remember that it takes time. Even if you set a goal now, it might take months or even years before you are actually able to achieve it, and that's okay. It's okay to take that time. It's okay for you to feel stuck or like you can't actually achieve what you are doing. But it's not okay to let that feeling hold you back. That is why you must set goals—and those goals must be specific enough to drive you forward as well. Your goals are important, and you will need to know what you can do to maintain them. Let's go over a few steps on how you can start setting a professional goal for yourself so you can be certain that you will succeed.

Step 1: Defining the Dream

What is it that you have always wanted out of life? Your dream job is not as impossible as you might think of it. It is not entirely impossible for you to achieve success if you know what you are doing and that is what this step is for. If you want to ensure that you can successfully get through everything, you will want to ensure that you look at your dream job as something that is possible.

You cannot achieve it, however, if you don't define it. You must be able to figure out what the goal is so you can get to it. Can you really get somewhere if you have nowhere in mind that you are going? Think about it—if you set your GPS up to guide you to the store, it will tell you exactly how to get there. That is because it has a defined location that it is directing you to. However, it cannot direct you if there is no goal in mind. If you do not input that ending point, it cannot function for you.

This is like your goals—you will need to define what you want if you want to be able to figure out how to get there. Think about what your dream is. Think back to what you used to want to do in childhood. How driven were you to be a great musician? An artist? A lawyer? Think back to that innocent time when you had something that you loved and wanted to do forever. Let that be part of your light that guides you. Write that down so you can access it later. This will help you to solidify it—you will have it seem that much more concrete when you have it in your face.

Step 2: Break it Down

When you know what you want, you can start to break it down further. You can start turning that long-term goal into short-term goals. Yes, you might want to be a doctor or a lawyer—but how do you get there? It can be fun to think long-term, but what about the shorter term? What is it that you will need to do short term to get that success that you are looking for? If you can plan out what you are doing, you should be able to find that success one way or another.

Maybe you write down that you will apply for law school. Or even go back a step—you will study for the LSAT so you can apply for law school. Breaking it down further will help you to figure out what you are doing and provide you with the ability to think about how to get to where you want.

Step 3: Make the Goals Measurable

When you have your intentional, incremental steps all lined out for yourself, it is time to start making your goals measurable. You need time limits for them so you can hold yourself accountable. You might say, for example, you will study for the LSAT for 30 minutes each night after dinner, before you get up to clean the dishes. You might say that you will apply to at least four jobs per week or that you will attend at least one networking event monthly. These are timed goals—they are set up to be measurable, so you have a clear goal in mind. This is imperative—it will help you to get that success that you really needed.

Step 4: The Action Plan

Finally, after you've started setting your goal, it is time to figure out your action plan. This can be difficult—it is hard to act on these goals that may, at times, seem utterly impossible, but it is good for you to understand them. It is good for you to recognize what you are doing and how you are doing it. If you want to be able to create those action plans, then you will need to be willing to follow the appropriate steps in the first place. We will be going over this later on in Step 3: Get a Game Plan. It is then that you will start building up that plan based on your goals, and it will be then that everything will really start coming to fruition.

Maintaining Motivation

Of course, if you are going to be trying to stick to your goals, you will need some degree of motivation that will help you with that. Setting goals is the easy part—achieving them is where the hard work comes in, and that is where you will really need to get to work. Unfortunately, a lack of motivation has killed a good deal of career goals, and because of that, you will need to banish this if you hope to be successful. Maintaining motivation requires you to recognize that there is no way that you can simply assume that the money will motivate you—you will have to find other levels of motivation that will help you as well. Maintaining motivation means that you must recognize that your goals are your own. It requires you to do your own thing for your own reasons without letting other people overwhelm or sway you.

Visualization

One method that many people swear by when it comes to maintaining motivation is visualization. This is the act of stopping and really seeing the result of your goals. It requires you to imagine yourself in that position of actually achieving what you have set out to do. It is highly powerful and beneficial and can help you immensely if you know what you are doing. All you will have to do is ensure that you are on track. Maintaining that motivation will help you. Imagine the feeling of relief or joy that you have after you've gotten through something. Imagine feeling utterly relieved or feeling like you are able to rest easy. This is what you need here—and it is highly beneficial to you. All you will need to do is find a way that you can really make it work for you.

Surround Yourself with Supportive People

Another tried, and true technique is to make sure that you are surrounded by people who will directly support and encourage you. If they are willing to see you as successful and worthy of that success, follow them. If they want to support you, allow them to. You need those cheerleaders around you, and they will help immensely. Positivity is contagious, and it can also be energizing. That positivity and people who believe in you will help you immensely.

Cut Out the Unsupportive Naysayers

And, if you are going to focus on primarily surrounding yourself with that positive support that you need, you will also need to ensure that you cut out the naysayers that might not actually help you the way that they should be. You want to ensure that anyone around you is actually beneficial to you and your success, and that means that you will have to cut out the people who are hurting your chances of getting it. If people think that you can't do something, then do it without them. Don't let them bring you down—just go forward on your own.

Get Accountable by Telling Other People About Your Goals

You could also try accountability. When you tell other people what it is that you are setting out to do, you effectively force yourself to have to follow through with them. When you tell people that you will do something, you will have to do it. This is simply due to the fact that people will ask you about it. You put yourself in a position where you are in the spotlight, and if you want to avoid having to tell people that you failed, you will have to follow through instead. This means that you will have to develop that ownership of your own failures if you do not succeed.

Of course, this method also works if you want to set up accountability buddies. By ensuring that people are on track with you, you will be able to see that ultimately, you will succeed. You will be able to effectively convince yourself that you need to do better because you are doing something alongside someone else. This trick is often used for people who want to work out at the gym but don't feel motivated. You can use it in a professional setting as well—you could work on a big project together, for example, or study together. This way, you have no choice but to feel like you have to keep going for the other person.

Chapter 2: Step 2 - Identifying Your Strengths and Weaknesses

If you want to develop in your career, there are a few other considerations that you will have to make along the way. One such consideration that you will have to consider is the strengths and weaknesses that you have. These different strengths and weaknesses that you have will dramatically change the way that you are able to engage in just about every job. They are what give you different degrees of success or struggles in various careers. If you want to be able to figure out what it is that you will do for yourself, you will

Being able to figure out the strengths and weaknesses that you have is a perfect way for you to begin understanding how to better yourself as well. If you are going to develop yourself, you will need to have a solid idea of where you are in the moment before anything else. You will need to recognize just how capable you are in the moment, so later on, you can work toward improvement. This will create your base reading of what you are doing—if you have that, you will then be capable of doing more.

Within this chapter, we are going to address a few key points. We will take a look at the power of self-awareness first, recognizing just how important it is. Then, it will be time to consider the strengths and weaknesses that you have. Finally, we will look at how your strengths can become a key factor in helping yourself to become capable of doing more. Through this process, you will be able to start working toward that desired development you were looking for.

The Power of Self-Awareness

Self-awareness is a soft skill that every person needs to have. In fact, it is a key factor in developing emotional intelligence. Emotional intelligence is important for being able to successfully engage with other people. The ability to focus on what you have to offer is highly important. Self-awareness will help you to improve your career thanks to the fact that it does a few different things: When you have that self-awareness, you can see yourself the way that other people see you. Additionally, you will be able to help yourself by recognizing your strengths and weaknesses.

Being self-aware and being emotionally self-aware, as well as aware of your skills, will help with the development of your career as well. You will be aware of the fact that you will need to change yourself. When you can see your weaknesses, you will see that there are areas that you will have to adjust your actions. Think about it—if you want to be able to develop your career further, you will need to start somewhere and the best starting point is to know what your strengths and weaknesses are so you can utilize them.

The self-awareness that you develop will also help you to work on the development of your leadership abilities as well. This is great—it is something that you will be able to use to your own benefit. Leadership is one of those abilities that you will need if you want to succeed in your career.

Additionally, you will discover that you can better understand other people with your self-awareness as well. The development of your people skills is another way that you can really get that benefit as well. Remember, many different employers prefer emotional intelligence and those people skills to experience. It is highly important—it helps greatly in the workplace.

Identifying Strengths

The first point we will consider is knowing your strengths. It is difficult to recognize what we are good at, but we are usually all too quick to talk about what we hate happily. This is a problem for many people—and if you want to figure out what your own strengths are, you will need to take the time to develop it. When you find the ability to identify your strengths, you will be able to begin utilizing them. Your strengths represent your best points—the parts of yourself that you can use to help yourself as well.

It will take some significant self-reflection for yourself to identify your strengths, but it is something that you will need to understand.

When you are complimented at work, what is it usually about? When someone comes to ask you for help, what do they want? These are important points to consider. Usually, people ask for help when they recognize that you are good at something. When you start to piece together what it is that you do well, you can use those points later on.

When it comes to identifying your strengths, there are a few points that you can use that will help you. These points are important for you to consider—they will help you to figure out where the points of strength are for yourself. These are:

1. Start by identifying what makes you tick. What is it that you love? What is it that you wish that you could do forever?
2. Figure out which things you do without trying very hard. What comes naturally to you?
3. Listen to what your heart says—do you have good emotions? What is it that you loved?

Together, these can be indicative of the strengths that you may have. They can help you immensely in the future. Make sure that you are well aware of what you are doing.

Identifying Weaknesses

You must also take the time to identify your weaknesses. The catch here is that your weaknesses are not disqualifying—not inherently, anyway. You can work a career if it is a weakness that you have—it will just require more effort. However, it is entirely possible. When it comes to figuring out your weaknesses, you usually have a pretty good idea. We're great at pointing out where we struggle.

Of course, you must be honest with yourself as well. You will need to tell yourself what it is that you can and cannot do without being biased. The key is in the natural lack of bias—you must be objective here. Without that objectivity, how are you supposed to succeed? How are you supposed to do well if you are afraid to admit what your weaknesses are?

Weaknesses are often areas where you simply haven't developed much—you may not be interested in them, or you may not care much about trying to do what you need to do. Weaknesses are often points where we suffer—we stay away from them. There are four key indicators that can help you to spot whether or not you actually are weak in something. These are:

1. You struggle to find any positivity or enjoyment in the activity—even when you are faced with having to complete it, you feel like it is more of a chore than anything else.
2. You may find that when it comes to completing that one activity, you are entirely uninterested, or you might try to do whatever you can to completely avoid it. You'd rather do almost anything else other than that one thing.

3. You get to what you have to do, but it takes you longer than it takes other people to complete whatever it is that you have done. You get stuck in trying over and over, but you really struggle to make it work for yourself.

4. You notice that when you do something, you struggle, and other people do much better than you do.

All of these are indicative of weakness. Remember, weaknesses aren't the end of the world—they are simply aspects of ourselves. We all have weaknesses, even if you cannot see them in someone else. We all have different skills that we struggle with, and because of that, you ought to have some compassion for yourself as well.

Using Your Strengths to Support Your Weaknesses

As you become more acquainted with your strengths and weaknesses, you can start to utilize them well. Your strengths can be used to overcome and support your weaknesses over time. You will be able to use them to find a way to overcome the problems that you may have otherwise. This is a fantastic way to utilize your strengths to their fullest extent.

For example, imagine that you struggle with networking. You hate having to go out of your way to talk to people. You don't like being forced to exchange pleasantries with other people. You might find that you are too shy or that talking to other people is too draining.

With all of that in mind, you might decide that ultimately, you need to change things somehow. Every time that you try to network, you feel yourself struggling. However, there are also ways that you can turn things around. You could, for example, find ways that your strengths can support the situation. For example, imagine that you struggle with networking—but you also are skilled at writing. Your ability to write becomes something that you can utilize for yourself to overcome that struggle with networking. You could instead work on sending emails or chatting with people to begin building that rapport before you have to meet people in person, allowing yourself to do a bit better when it comes time to actually engage.

By taking your strengths to use them to support the weaknesses, you will be able to start taking advantage of them. You can utilize your strengths, and by doing so, you help yourself avoid running into problems. When you do this over time, you realize that you can help yourself—you can prevent yourself from running into problems. This is a perfect way that you can build your skills so you will be able to better develop your career further.

Think about it—if you find that there are struggles with your career in certain aspects, you may find that you have to overcome it somehow. This is something that you can do with ease. You just have to know what you are doing. Push your strengths so you can be certain that you are on top of them at all times. If you can do this, you will start to encourage yourself to do better.

Chapter 3: Step 3 - Get a Game Plan

At this point, you should have a pretty solid idea of the general direction that you want to go. Now, it's time to work out the plans that you will need to make it happen. At this point, it's time to figure out what it is that you want to do. It is time to figure out the right way that you should be working with yourself to make your plan actually come to fruition. If you want to be able to successfully develop your career, you are in for the long haul, and it will take time and effort to make it come to fruition.

Building a career plan that will work for you involves figuring out what it is that you want and then working to make it happen. Of course, only so much of anything at any given point in time is within your control, and that means that you also have to accept a lack of control in things that you cannot. When you do this and remember to keep your focus where it matters, you should be able to see your game plan clearly in front of you. You will be able to pursue your game plan and stay on that path to success if you know what you are doing. Ultimately, being able to do so will help you to figure out how to navigate the world around you. It will help you to stick to your success.

Create a Purpose Statement

Our first step to finding a game plan is setting up your purpose statement. When you do this, you start by figuring out what your goal is, which we discussed earlier. Your purpose statement is supposed to embody what happens in your goal. It should show you what you need to do and how you need to do it. It will help you to figure out what it is that you need to do and how you can do it. The sooner that you figure out how to do so, the better.

So, take your goal. Set it up so that you can frame it as a purpose statement and use that statement proudly. When you use your statement on a regular basis, you will find yourself successfully keeping yourself on track to head right for your game plan, whatever it may be. Through setting up your purpose statement, you help to keep your focus right where it is supposed to be, and you help yourself to celebrate exactly what it is that you want to do or be.

Even better, write your mission statement somewhere that you will be able to access regularly. Put it somewhere that you will see on a regular basis. One commonplace that people like to put theirs is on their mirrors, or they like to quote their statement on their phone's lock screen, so they see them regularly. This little reminder is a great way to have that little morale boost, even when things get tough.

Focus, Focus, Focus

The next part of your game plan is all about focus. You need to identify several different points that you must make a priority in your own career. Is there a certain specialty that you want to look into? Are there certain aspects of your career that you want to focus on? Are there certain career paths that you wish to follow in particular? When you focus on your career development and recognize that your career goals matter, and choose to focus on them, you will find yourself much more capable of being able to navigate through the situations that you are in.

Through ensuring that you follow these different tasks and making sure that you are constantly following along with what you would potentially need to do, you should find yourself succeeding with ease. You just have to know what you are doing and make sure that you hone that focus while you still can. Don't let small inconveniences knock you off track. Didn't you get that promotion you were going for? Too bad—but don't let that keep you from the successes that you deserve. You can and will be able to achieve the true successes that you've been looking for.

Control What You Can

As you work on that career game plan, make sure that you don't extend it too far. This means that you need to focus on what you know that you can control. Pay special attention to the ways that you know that you can successfully get through a situation on your won. Take the time to figure out how to navigate through these situations without causing yourself problems. Make sure that your game plan for your career is something that is entirely within your control. If you are constantly trying to focus on aspects of your career that you cannot control, you are going to end up making yourself miserable as you constantly try to get the results that you want.

Figuring out what you can and cannot control becomes imperative if you want to be able to be the person that you want to be. Through looking at only the things that you control, you can take that power back. You remember that ultimately, you are in charge and in control. That control is exactly what you are looking to remember.

Focus on the Future

Finally, you want to make sure that your game plan is focused on the future. Where do you want yourself to end up? What do you want to end up doing? When you want to be able to succeed, you start by finding that focus on the future and what you want to end up doing. If you can do this, you should find yourself successfully getting to it.

Your game plan should look toward the future that you are looking for. What is it that you want to achieve? What is it that you hope to do? And what are the steps to getting there? If you want to get to that point in your life, you will have to be able to break it down into little, manageable steps that you know that you will be able to maintain.

For example, perhaps your plan is that you want to become a lawyer. What are the steps that it will take you to get there?

Maybe you are currently just a receptionist in a law firm, but you know that is where you want to get to. You might find yourself sitting down and telling yourself that you have to do certain things to get there. You will need to, for example, make sure that you take the LSAT to prepare for law school. Then you have to be admitted to law school and attend your classes. After that, you have to pass your classes, and pass your bar exam, and then *finally,* you still have to get hired working for a law firm or start up your own practice. There are steps that you have to follow if you want to be able to achieve that end goal of being an attorney, and by making sure that you schedule yourself and your plans in this manner, you will find yourself being more capable of actively achieving that goal.

Throughout that entire time of working through law school in the example, you would need to spend a long while—years, even—working toward that goal. You will have to spend hours studying and volunteering. You will have to memorize all sorts of different laws and codes, and in the end, you achieve your goal. That game plan that you develop will help you to keep yourself on track because it will provide you with the motivation that you are looking for.

Chapter 4: Step 4 - Network, Network, Network!

From there, the next consideration to make is the idea of networking. Being a successful networker matters immensely. It will help you to ensure that at the end of the day, you can and will be able to get those references that you will need in all sorts of different positions to ensure that you will be the person that you want to be.

If you want to be able to network, you will need to find the right people, but you will also want to have the right skills. You need to balance everything out so that you get the results that you are looking for. You want to make sure that you've got the opportunity to connect to other people because, in terms of your career, you never know when it might be useful.

Keep in mind that when you refer to networking, you really are just talking about building relationships. There is nothing particularly different about the creation of business and personal relationships other than the degree of professionalism that is expected. You might be drinking buddies with your best friend, but you would most likely not be drinking buddies with your mentor or your advisor. With that in the forefront of your mind, it is time to look at the ways that you can get through what you are doing yourself and how networking works.

The Importance of Networking

Networking is all about creating long-term relationships with other people, but the catch is, they must be mutually beneficial. You and the other person that you are working with must both be benefitting somehow from your relationship, and that adds a degree of authenticity to the relationship that allows for the successful networking that you are attempting to achieve. When you do this the right way, you should develop trust and rapport with the people that you are attempting to connect to in the first place. This is essential.

Networking events and opportunities are everywhere. From getting coffee to choosing to talk to people at a meeting, or even sending a quick email to someone to let them know that you were thinking of them when you were looking at something, you will see that you have a whole multitude of different ways that you can connect. Networking can happen just about anywhere and with just about anyone—it is all about building those connections that you choose to foster and develop.

Typically, the most connected people are the most successful just due to the fact that you have the connections that you need to have all the right resources for what you want to do. If you want or need something and you have a wide network, there is a good chance that you will have someone that is able to help you. You will have people that can help you when you need it, and in return, you will be able to mentor other people at the same time. This is essential—being able to relate to other people and connect in these manners is exactly what you will need to do, and it will help you immensely.

Creating a Network

Your network should be diverse and varied. There should be people from all sorts of different fields, positions, and backgrounds there to help you. You never know when you need a mechanic, a landscaper, a lawyer, or a dermatologist. Because you never know who you will need to help you in the future or where people will be in the future, one of the best approaches is to genuinely connect with everyone around you. When you do this, recognizing that you and those around you can all offer each other something of value, you will start to build up those relationships that will become the professional ones that you will need.

Keep in mind that there is no one-size-fits-all approach to networking the right way. All sorts of people will have all sorts of different aspects that they want to consider or attempt when networking, and you will need to figure out which the right one for you is. It will take time and effort, plus some patience and experimentation, but if you do this, you will eventually find what works well for you. Find your own networking style. Do you prefer to be one on one with people? Do you prefer networking in groups with plenty of people to meet? Either way, you will need that connection to those around you, and you will need to find a way to line up with everyone there that you are working with in a way that will work for you.

When you network, one of the most important things to remember is that you are trying to connect with people. This means that you are working to further your relationships with them before you choose to benefit yourself. You should always be in a position to benefit the people that you want to network with in order to get along well and foster those relationships the right way.

Then, after you do something to help them, the next thing that you should consider doing is choose to follow up. Make sure that, no matter what you are doing or how you are doing it, you follow up accordingly. You need to make sure that you are relating directly to the people that you are trying to keep in your network, and that means following up regularly. You don't need to send a novel—just a quick message saying that you were happy to meet them and that you look forward to connecting again in the future, or a quick thank you for doing something that benefitted you.

Remember that it is never the wrong time to invest in your network. It is always the right time to work to make those connections to other people so that you will be able to thrive. It is always the right time to reach out and connect to others, and it is always the right time to find a way to be able to connect honestly and authentically. All you have to do is get out there and try. After all, the only real mistake with networking is simply not networking at all.

Chapter 5: Step 5 - Take All Opportunities

The opportunities presented to your matter. If you don't take the ones that you've got available to you, how are you ever going to make the progress that you are looking for? How are you ever going to actually get anywhere if you never bother trying to take what is right there? Taking your situation for granted is a fantastic way to end up wasting time and energy rather than ever actually progressing. If you don't take opportunities when they present themselves, you are going to remain stagnant in life. This is true in your career, in your general life, and in your situation as well. Ultimately, being able to take all opportunities matters immensely and will help you to get exactly where you are supposed to be.

The opportunities that appear before you matter and will help you. Of course, it's hard to take literally every single one, but you should always try to get the ones that appear before you. You may have the opportunity to attend a new event at work. You may find yourself wondering if you have the opportunity to ask for help if you are struggling—and if you do, you should take it. These opportunities are ripe for the taking, almost dangling in front of you, but if you never do so, you will never get as far as someone who does.

By remembering not to pass up things you shouldn't, you can watch your career advance. If someone told you that they would pay for you to get that advanced degree, would you take them up on the offer? If someone told you that they would give you $50,000 for making a few simple changes now that would completely alter the path that you are on in the future, would you do it? Most people like to say yes… But the truth is, too many people skip the opportunities that are presented to them.

Why We Pass Up Things, We Shouldn't

When you avoid taking opportunities, you trap yourself in mediocrity. You hold yourself back ad that will be the bane of your existence. By avoiding the things that matter and by passing up on the things that you should have access to, you end up putting yourself in a position where you cannot get anywhere. You end up in a position where you are going to struggle immensely, and that is a huge problem. By not taking opportunities, you are practically asking to be left where you are without any sort of progress. You are asking to be held back without being able to move forward because you simply won't take the next logical step.

We do this for all sorts of reasons, but the biggest one is fear. If you are someone who is anxious or afraid of what will happen if you suddenly take an opportunity, you are going to be held back no matter what you try to do, and that is not an okay situation to be in. If you do this, you are going to find yourself struggling. You are going to find yourself in a position where you cannot take care of anything, and that is going to hold you back immensely.

The fear of the unknown needs to be defeated. If you want to take an opportunity, you have to take a chance, and if you are not willing to take a chance, you are not willing to make the progress that you will need. Ultimately, being able to do so matters. It will help you to get what you are looking for. It will help you to figure out what you are doing and where you are going in life.

You will have to take control of your life and your fear. You will have to tell yourself that you are no longer afraid. You have to tell yourself that you are no longer going to fall for these bad habits and that you are going to find a way to succeed. Let go of that fear and turn toward opportunities. Become the opportunistic person that you can—and that is meant in a good way. If an opportunity appears in front of you, you should always take it. It will be the key to your success.

The Power of Opportunity

Opportunities are incredibly powerful. Your opportunities are there to propel you forward. Each and every opportunity is like a fork in the path of life. Every time that you come to an opportunity, whether due to luck or due to skill, you need to make a choice. You need to choose between taking the opportunity and letting yourself stay on the path that you are on. By doing this, you will be able to make yourself work harder. You will be able to benefit from you. You will find ways that you can get through your life just by making those simple choices.

What would you do if, through your networking, you suddenly found yourself trying to figure out how you could do better? What would you do if you suddenly had a new career path in front of you that you could take, but you had no idea if it was going to work? You might not know whether that career is going to get you any further— but the truth is, that's okay. It's okay to be afraid. The only thing that you will need to do is take those chances. Take those opportunities. Grab them, and move forward.

Taking Opportunities When Offered

If you're looking for options to start taking opportunities, you will see that you are more than capable of success. You will be able to figure out what you could do if you were to take opportunities just by being willing to try. If you're ready to boost your opportunity taking abilities, try following several of these options for you. Each of these different smaller actions will help you to be the successful person that you want to be, and all you will have to do is make an effort to begin.

1. *Say Yes:* Just by saying yes when someone asks you to do something, you will begin taking more opportunities. If you

find yourself talking to someone at the café, only to have them tell you that they'd like to meet up with you again to discuss some potential career-related opportunities, tell them yes. Tell them that you are more than willing to do so. Tell them that you are entirely happy to do so and that you want to be that successful person that you want to be. This helps you to stop passing by opportunities that might be incredibly lucrative but scare you. By remembering to take those chances when you can, you will be able to do better. You will take more of those chances, and you will take more opportunities. You might be surprised to see where you end up.

2. ***Don't Hesitate:*** Hesitation is that feeling of apprehension before you answer. It is letting fear get the better of you. However, keep in mind that opportunities in life are short. They are not there forever, and you can't waste time when it comes to trying to pursue them. Don't hold yourself back because you are afraid. Commit and move on. Remember that the opportunities in front of you are not always exclusive, and if you aren't careful, you can end up costing yourself time and money. Someone else might take that opportunity before you do it if you hesitate.

3. ***Take Risks:*** Risks aren't necessarily a bad thing. In fact, risks are fantastic options for you. When you take a risk, you will find yourself working harder, and you will also find yourself

getting rewards back when you least expect them. Most opportunities will always present themselves when you take a chance. Maybe you look around and tell yourself that you cannot possibly talk to that person at the networking event because they won't help you anyway. You just let fear take control of your situation. You just allowed yourself to be controlled by something that should not have had that power over you in the first place. So, what do you do then? You take risks! The opportunities that present themselves to your matter—and the best ones are those that come when you do something risky. Remember this—you have to kick those opportunities into existence by taking risks, but if you do so, you should succeed.

4. *Positivity:* When you have a positive attitude, you will attract more opportunities as well. This idea of positivity will attract other people to you, and because of that, you will have more options in the future. Additionally, people who are positive tend to also be more willing to take a risk because they see the positive sides in what they do. Remember to stick to the positive thinking, and the risks in front of you should fade away relatively quickly

5. *Network More:* Opportunities present themselves to you because you have these opportunities. Through networking and meeting more people, you up the chances that you will have an

opportunity to present itself just due to the fact that you will be able to use them. You will be able to present yourself better to others, and you may even find that you've got people in your network that can actually help open the door to some new opportunities that you otherwise would not have had in front of you, meaning that you may find yourself getting further just by knowing the right people.

6. *Stay Curious:* When you remain curious, you keep your mind active. You will ask questions to people that you naturally want to answer. And, eventually, you may even ask questions that others don't. This can help you to pave the way to new opportunities just by virtue of opening a new line of consideration. If you just asked a question about how something would work that no one had considered before, you will open those lines of communication.

7. *Focus:* Make sure that you keep your eyes on the prize. Know where your ultimate goal is, and stay on the lookout for anything that will allow you to get there. If you know where you want to be in a few years and you see the option to start moving toward it, you should find that you can successfully get to them. You just need to figure out how you can get to it. This will help you determine whether you should get there and whether you should pass up opportunities that just aren't going to get you there. Imagine that you have a chance to go to a

prestigious med school… But you want to be a chef. That option isn't going to help you get very far when it isn't what you had wanted in the first place, and that means that you would be wasting time and money. By knowing where you are going in life, the path that you will need to get there will open up little by little.

Chapter 6: Step 6 - Be Accountable

Accountability matters. By being accountable for yourself and your work, staying on top of it all, you will need to make sure that you balance everything yourself. How do you manage to do this without anyone else breathing down your neck? How do you make this progress if you don't know where you are going or why? What can you do if you need to get through everything? The answer is simple— you need to build yourself up that accountability.

In most workplaces, you have the manager there to keep you accountable. They breathe down your neck and make sure that you are on track, or they threaten you with consequences. They will make it impossible for you to get away without doing anything that you should be. However, the truth is, you need to figure out a way that you can start making that progress for yourself. Think about the ways that you can hold yourself accountable in your entire career. You might have that manager keeping you accountable in your one job, but if you want to get further in your career, how are you going to get there? What are you going to do to make sure that you can find that final position that you want to be in? The truth is simple: You become accountable to yourself. When you can do that for yourself, you realize that you can maintain yourself and stay on track. You need to maintain your own accountability and follow how you can manage yourself.

Create a Mission Statement

Remembering to have your own personal mission statement helps you to keep your eyes on why you do what you do. It is incredibly easy to get lost in the forest and see only the trees as you go through life on a daily basis, especially if you have a job that is highly repetitive. However, if you were to work harder and figure out how you can maintain that success that you are looking for, you should find that you can actually get significantly further in life. What is motivating you? Don't say money or success—we all want those things. For most people, they have a reason for what they are doing. A doctor's personal mission statement may be to help people regardless of who they are, saving lives, and promoting healing in the world. A lawyer may be there to seek justice for every person, regardless of who they are.

Teachers may tell themselves that they are there to educate a new generation to ensure that they know what they are doing and how they can get to where they need to be in life. These mission statements matter—they are ways that you will be able to get through everything. They will remind you to see the bigger picture, even if you are grading your 50th paper of the day, or if you are once again listening to someone cough to tell them that they've got the common cold. By remembering these things and looking at how you can change up what you are doing and how you are interacting with others, you will help yourself remain accountable because you will never lose sight of what matters to you and why you went the way that you did in life. The personal mission statement will keep you on track.

Lists

By making lists, you can keep track of what you need to do and why. You will be able to remind yourself of everything that you need to do at any point in time and remind yourself that they matter. When you go through these lists, you will find that you are told that you need to change up what you are doing and why. You will show yourself that you will be capable of doing what you have to do, and you will be able to get through it all because you can see that list of things in front of you.

Every morning, or every night before bed, create a list of things that you need to do for the day, and you will be able to manage yourself so much more successfully if you do. You will be able to figure out how best to work through these situations just by virtue of having the resources in front of you. The sooner that you can get through this all, the sooner you will be able to do better. You can even break down your lists into smaller, more manageable lists by type of activity to help yourself further.

Reward Yourself for Successes

As you get through the tasks that you complete, you can't forget to reward yourself. Think about it—managers will reward good employees by thanking them and praising them. Some managers will even give bonuses for doing a good job. However, if you are managing yourself and needing to keep yourself accountable, you will need to complete your own personal steps to success as well. You will need to think about the ways that you can reward yourself as you succeed, and you will need to follow through with it.

Rewards make us more willing to complete something, so if you reward yourself with time or with something nice because you got through your work, you will find yourself more successful. This is imperative to your own personal successes—it will help you to figure out what you are doing and why. It will show you the way to get through everything that you need to do and how you can get through it all. Ultimately, offer yourself a reward for completing those to-do lists, even if it is as simple as treating yourself with something nice.

One Task at a Time

You must also remember to complete tasks one thing at a time. While we all like to think that we are great multitaskers, the truth is, the human brain is not built to do so. The human brain is meant to focus on just one task at a time, and by trying to multitask, you really are just making things harder for yourself and causing yourself future problems. When you are trying to be accountable, then you will need to make sure that you actually focus on those individual things that you are doing.

Working on things one at a time will allow you to put all of your concentration on one thing so you can complete it faster. It will allow you to make that progress that you are looking for quicker, and it will help you to get through everything on your to-do list quicker than you could have imagined.

For example, what if you need to get through some work? One of the best ways that you can do so is to check your emails at set times during the day instead of every time they come in. This is a good way to ensure that you can and will be able to get control. When you do this effectively, you should find yourself getting further than you thought. Close your door and focus. Goals will be met sooner and easier if you focus rather than trying to stretch yourself thin by going several different directions at the same time.

Emphasize Your Strengths While Supporting Weaknesses

You, like everyone else in the world, are born knowing how to do very little. We all have to learn to do things around us. We all have to learn to focus, to properly get through the things that we will need to do. We all have to find ways that we can emphasize our skills. We will all have natural strengths and weaknesses, and the best people at keeping themselves accountable are able to emphasize their strengths while supporting their weaknesses. When you can do this for yourself, you can find ways that you are able to do more.

For example, maybe you are great at writing—but you struggle to actually have a one-on-one conversation and stay on track. You can get around this by emphasizing that strength of writing—just choose to work in ways that you will show yourself what matters. Tell yourself that you can do better by emailing people about important factors rather than trying to do it in person.

You should actively be looking for ways that you can take the skills that you have so that you can support those weaknesses that you've got. If you can do this the right way, you can remind yourself of how you can begin to support those weaknesses. Don't be embarrassed by them—we all have weaknesses in life. But what you can do is make sure that you show yourself that you can get past them yourself. All you have to do is be willing to show yourself a success.

Chapter 7: Step 7 - Always Strive for Better

Aristotle famously said, "We are what we repeatedly do. Excellence, therefore, is not an act but a habit." What this means for you is that if you want to be excellent and if you want to get yourself further in your own personal career path, you will need to strive for it. You can't be comfortable with where you are. You can't be stagnant—you have to push yourself forward so you can be the person that you want to be. When you strive for better, you can help yourself to become that successful person that you wish to be. When you strive for excellence in your own life and in your own career, you will see it beginning to manifest for you, and you will start to have those new career opportunities arising in front of you. You just have to know how to take them.

Now, this doesn't mean that you are looking for perfection. No—perfection is unattainable. But what you are looking for is to see constant improvement. You are looking to see yourself actively working on getting better, do better, and be better. You are looking at the ways that you can find yourself successfully getting through everything that you will need to do and seeing the ways that you will be able to do so. Ultimately, those successes are built upon being able to successfully get through everything that you are looking for. You just have to be willing to find a way to make it happen.

Read Daily

Take the time to read something new every single day. Preferably, this should be about something related to your career. Take the time to research and learn something new just because you can. Learning and reading will always work to up your skills, and you also exercise your brain while you do so, meaning that you will be giving yourself that added boost that you were looking for just by virtue of reading. If you want to be a better, well-rounded person with the opportunity for success, you need to figure out what you can do to make these happen.

Make Car Time Productive

Another way that you can strive for excellence is to start using that time that you have where you might not actually think much about what you can do and make it productive. How long is your commute? In the United States, the average American travels 26 minutes each way to work, and most people will travel up to 1.5 hours away to their jobs if they pay well enough. What does this mean for you? It means that you may have anywhere from 1 to 3 hours of free time if you are like the average American, where you are sitting in your car. Make that time productive. Instead of simply sitting in the car, listening to the morning talk show, consider playing podcasts and audiobooks about topics that you want to learn more about. Listen to the people in your field that you know is successful and allow yourself to follow their advice.

By making car time productive, you reclaim a lot of work and time that otherwise would have been completely wasted by you and you can use that work time to be the successful person that you want to be. You just have to be willing to hold onto it and make use of it.

Focus on Bettering Yourself

By constantly focusing on ways that you can do better for yourself, you will strive for excellence. You should always be looking for ways at work that you can do more. Look for how you can streamline the process of what your career currently is. Work on becoming better at your job and being able to be more productive. As you do so, mastering the skills in front of you, you can naturally begin to take on those other tasks that will help you further your career path even further. Even surgeons have to learn little by little. Yes, they practice in med school and yes, they practice on cadavers sometimes, but that isn't the same as going into a human body to repair it. They have to start small, mastering simple basics such as suturing before they can start getting to the bigger, more complex surgeries. The best surgeons in their fields weren't there just because they were prodigies in school—they had to learn and hone their skills over the years to get to where they are.

Focusing on how you can continue to better yourself and your career will help you to figure out how you can get to where you really want to be in life. It will help you to figure out how you can continue to develop your own career and improve as you do so. The more that you do this, the more likely that you are to ever actually get to those end goals that you have set for yourself. Keep that focus where it belongs and always strive to be better at something. If your last best time was an hour to complete something, start trying to do it in 55 minutes instead. This kind of thing, changing gup how you do what you need to do and working hard to make it happen the right way, will help you.

Always Set a New Goal

Another way that you can help yourself is to remember that you should always be setting those new goals in life. Don't let yourself be held back by not having a goal—figure out what you can do to get that new goal rolling. If you've just completed a goal that you were trying to meet, it is time for you to start figuring out how you can do better. It is time for you to start figuring out where it is that you want to go next so you can strive for it.

By constantly moving the goalposts for yourself, you will keep striving for more. You will not be aiming for perfection—you will be aiming for excellence, and that difference is what is important. Every time that you get to your last goal figure out what the next logical step is and take that as well. The more that you do this, the quicker you will realize that you can and will be able to get to where you want to be. This is imperative if you want to be successful, and it will help you immensely.

Be Proud

Don't forget that when you do something, you should be proud of your results. You should always strive to present something that you can take pride in. If you've completed a new project, is it done to the point that you are proud? Are you able to comfortably say that you tried your best and that you are happy with how it came out? If so, then great! If not, why not? Why are you putting out work that you are not proud of? You want to learn what you can do to better the situation, and you want to learn how you can do better in the future as well. However, if you embrace this understanding of constantly striving to be proud of the work that you do, you will be naturally pushing your career in the direction that you want it to go. You will get that success where you want it somewhere along the way, and that success can be embraced. It was well-earned.

Conclusion

We never get to the end of the road when we are constantly paving it in front of us. You want to show yourself that you are constantly trying to do better with yourself and your career, and hopefully this guide has helped you with that.

As you are heading out to develop your own career, whether you are just starting out or you have been working on your career for years at this point, you know now that there are certain things that you need to maintain and keep in mind. You know that there are certain ways that you will be able to do better. You can see that you are constantly working to better yourself and to better the people around you. Ultimately, being able to follow your career path will help you to achieve the successes that you have been looking for and all you have to do is keep that forward momentum. You can do it! You've got the drive. You have the skills and the passion—you just have to hone it and keep pushing forward.

From here, remember that you have the power to better yourself. Remember that you are striving for excellence here—not perfection. Let go of the feeling that you need perfection to thrive. Let go of the idea that you will only be successful if you are perfect, and remember to look at yourself for what you are: A constant work in progress. Your career is one of your biggest works in progress that you will ever have and when you embrace that point, you will find that getting to that success is far easier than you probably anticipated and that matters immensely. That change in your thinking and that recognition is the aspect that you are missing to succeed in life, and if you can get it, you will find yourself succeeding.

More by Theodore Kingsley

Discover all books from the Career Development Series by Theodore Kingsley at:

bit.ly/theodore-kingsley

Book 1: How to Write a Resume

Book 2: How to Write a Cover Letter

Book 3: How to Find a Job

Book 4: How to Prepare for Job Interviews

Book 5: How to Brand Yourself

Book 6: How to Network

Book 7: How to Develop Your Career

Book 8: How to Change Careers

Themed book bundles available at discounted prices:

bit.ly/theodore-kingsley

Printed in the USA
CPSIA information can be obtained
at www.ICGtesting.com
LVHW020006300923
759626LV00004B/230